Reading Body Language

The Art & Science of Decoding Nonverbal Communication

By: Dana Williams

ALL RIGHTS RESERVED

No part of this book may be reproduced, stored in a retrieval system, or transmitted in any form or by any means, electronic, mechanical, photocopying, recording, scanning, or otherwise, without the prior written permission of the publisher.

Limit of Liability/Disclaimer of Warranty: the publisher and the author make no representations or warranties with respect to the accuracy or completeness of the contents of this work and specifically disclaim all warranties, including without limitation warranties of fitness for a particular purpose. No warranty may be created or extended by sales or promotional materials. The advice and strategies contained herein may not be suitable for every situation. This work is sold with the understanding that the publisher is not engaged in rendering medical, legal or other professional advice or services. If professional assistance is required, the services of a competent professional person should be sought. Neither the publisher nor the author shall be liable for damages arising therefrom. The fact that an individual, organization or website is referred to in this work as a citation and/or potential source of further information does not mean that the author or the publisher endorses the information the individuals, organization or website may provide or recommendations they/it may make. Further, readers should be aware that websites listed on this work may have changed or disappeared between when this work was written and when it is read.

TABLE OF CONTENTS

INTRODUCTION 4

CHAPTER ONE WHAT IS BODY LANGUAGE AND WHY IT MATTERS 6

CHAPTER TWO THE BODY LANGUAGE OF A BABY 12

CHAPTER THREE THE BODY LANGUAGE OF A TODDLER .. 19

CHAPTER FOUR THE BODY LANGUAGE OF A CHILD 27

CHAPTER FIVE THE BODY LANGUAGE OF A TEENAGER 38

CHAPTER SIX BODY LANGUAGE IN LOVE AND MARRIAGE 49

CHAPTER SEVEN BODY LANGUAGE BETWEEN FRIENDS…OR ARE THEY FOES? 62

CHAPTER EIGHT BODY LANGUAGE IN THE WORKPLACE .. 88

CHAPTER NINE BODY LANGUAGE AS A MEANS OF SELF-DEFENSE 104

CHAPTER TEN CULTURAL DIFFERENCES IN BODY LANGUAGE 116

CHAPTER ELEVEN HOMOPHONES AND HOMOGRAPHS IN BODY LANGUAGE 136

CLOSING COMMENTS 145

INTRODUCTION

I recently heard a friend of mine recount an event that took place while attending a graveside service for a family member—one at which masks were optional. She said that after the service was over, someone (wearing a mask) came up to her and said, "I'm so sorry for your loss. I never met your uncle, but I've heard so many stories about him from your cousin that I felt like I knew him well."

My friend went on to say that it was several hours later before she realized who it was she had been speaking to behind the mask. "It was crazy," she said. "I didn't have a clue who I was talking to at the time. I knew I *should* know, but I didn't. Part of the reason was because I wasn't expecting her to be there. But part of it was because it's incredibly difficult to recognize people wearing a mask."

She's right. It is hard to recognize people we don't know very well or those we don't see on a regular basis. But more than that, it is harder than ever to read people—to see what they mean, to pick up on their mood and interpret the context of their words.

We can't blame mask wearing for everything we miss when it comes to reading body language. More often than not when we misinterpret someone's body language it's due to a lack of focus or false assumptions.

The study of body language has been the topic of countless studies and experiments in sociology, psychology, psychiatry, biology, and human behavior studies such as relationship counseling, trauma recovery, and stress reduction. There's also that element of just wanting to know where you stand with someone. You're not wanting to waste your time in a relationship while also becoming more self-aware so that you send the right message and leave people with the impression you want them to be left with.

That is what this book is designed to help you do. We're going to do a deep dive into what body language is, what to look for, how to read someone's body language, and how to translate the different dialects of body language.

So, get comfy, grab a cup of coffee, be ready to take a few notes (mental or otherwise), and keep your laptop handy so you can 'analyze' what people are saying in some of the photos you've taken.

CHAPTER ONE
WHAT IS BODY LANGUAGE AND WHY IT MATTERS

"People may not remember what you said, but they will remember how you made them feel."
~ Maya Angelou

Body language is defined as: **the communication of personal feeling, emotions, attitude, and thoughts through facial expressions, body movements, and posture/positioning.**

The term 'body language' is somewhat deceptive, however, because technically it isn't a language at all. No words—written or spoken are involved—so the word 'language' is a technical error. The more appropriate term would be *body communication*. But since some say *'tomAto'* and some say 'tomato,' we're not going to squabble over semantics. Body language it will be.

As for what body language actually does, there are three distinct purposes that have been identified as belonging to body language:

1: A conscious replacement for speech.

More than a few moms have been credited with having 'The Look'—the one that brings her children into immediate and silent submission. For some moms, the look is a plastic smile that is really saying, "Everyone else may think you're being cute, but I don't, and my opinion is the one that matters." For other moms, it's the stare/glare that has the power to shoot flaming arrows from their eyes if the child those arrows are aimed at doesn't stop what they are doing immediately. And for other moms, it's the tilted head with the guilt-trip sigh that can pierce the heart of the most stubborn child.

There is nothing unintentional about these looks. In fact, just the opposite is true. Few things are *more* intentional than 'the look.' But death stares and guilt trips aren't the only conscious forms of body language. A puffed-out chest, arms crossed in front of you, standing stiff with your feet square with your shoulders, or leaning in toward someone with one foot in front of the other are all ways to say, "I mean business, so don't cross me." But it's not all bad. There are plenty of ways for your body to speak a language of friendship, affection, and love. Smiles, open arms, hugs, a tender touch on the shoulder or cheek, and a playful nudge to the ribs all have plenty of nice things to say.

The intentional use of body language can speak when it is inappropriate to speak out loud. The intentional use of body language can also speak when you don't know what to say. For example, when you wish to express your concern and sympathies to someone who has lost a loved one, but you just cannot find the right words. Or maybe you want to send a message to your child from the bleachers to the baseball diamond, soccer field, or basketball court. You know they would shrink from embarrassment if you hollered something out loud, but at the same time, they send more than one look your way knowing you'll give them that thumbs up or nod of approval.

One of the most beloved and famous examples of this is comedienne Carol Burnett's weekly message to her grandma. The infamous tug on the ear. Carol, who had been raised by her grandma, tugged on her ear at the end of every show as a way to say, "I love you, Grandma." She did it every week as she told her audience goodnight, as long as her grandma was alive.

Do you do anything like that? Do you and your spouse, kids, or friends have any body language 'code words'? If so, how does it make you feel to receive those looks and touches? Or to give them and know what it means to the one you are giving them to? Do these wordless words make you feel all warm and fuzzy? Do they give you the boost of confidence you need? Have they been the not-so-little extra you need to get you through a tough time? Have you been able to make someone special feel a little less alone knowing you were there and aware?

2: A means to reinforce speech.

Using body language as a way of reinforcing your words is something we do both consciously and subconsciously. Conscious movements and gestures are used to stress a point we want to make, to put people at ease, to verify our authority, and to demonstrate or reveal our sense of confidence or submission. It's the body's way of putting something in italics or bold print.

Examples of consciously reinforcing speech using body language:

- Pointing a finger at someone when you reprimand or discipline them.

- Furrowing or raising our eyebrows to emphasize our displeasure or surprise.
- A quick nod of the head to unconditionally declare our affirmation of something or to punctuate our 'so be it' or 'that's the way it's going to be.'
- Smiling or smiling and gently nodding to reassure someone.
- A gentle touch to the shoulder brings added comfort, condolence, affection, and a reminder that says, "You've got this."
- A slow nod of the head or handshake is a conscious way to show submission, agreement, or reconciliation.

Subconscious reinforcement is done for the same reasons as conscious reinforcement. Subconscious reinforcement of speech using body language consists of those things we do out of habit, i.e., without thinking. The most common one I can think of is someone who uses their hands when they talk. Think about it—how many times have you heard someone say, or have *you* said, "If I couldn't use my hands I couldn't talk"? But that's not the only one. Some of the others include shaking or nodding the head to indicate how sure you are of something or to emphasize the level of conviction or certainty you have about something. Using your hands and arms to indicate the size of something is also a way to reinforce your speech using body language.

3: A subconscious mirror or betrayer of mood.

The subconscious reflects what is really going on inside. It doesn't know how to wear a mask or pull the wool over anyone's eyes. The subconscious is like the preschooler who is brutally but innocently honest. It isn't afraid to say, "You look ridiculous in that outfit." Or "I'm going to go far...just try and stop me!"

Subconscious body language can be as subtle as standing up nice and straight, which tells everyone you are confident and not the kind of person to back down from a challenge.

There are multiple ways body language mirrors or betrays our mood...

- Looking away from the person talking to you mirrors your lack of interest in that person.
- Tight lips to signal displeasure, worry, or frustration.
- Clenched fists indicate you are trying to hold your tongue and not respond angrily.
- Tapping your foot or drumming your fingers on the table/desk are both sure signs of impatience.
- Biting your nails, twisting your hair, or biting your lower lip says, "I'm nervous" in every language.

These are just a few examples of the different reasons we use body language. And just to 'prove' how on-target these examples are, do the following:

- Have a face-to-face conversation with at least three people today.
- Bite the bullet and watch the news.

While you are doing each of these things, pay close attention to the other person's hand movements, posture, and facial expressions. Do they mirror and match the words coming out of their mouths?

And what about you? Pay close attention to what you do in the course of the conversations you have with others. Do you do anything different based on the closeness of your relationship with them? For example, do you stand closer to one than the other(s)? Do you smile more? Do you physically put yourself on their level by stooping or sitting? Or do you stand over them to establish control or authority—consciously or subconsciously?

Now here are three final questions for you before we move on: What impression do these people (both in person and on the screen) make on you? What impression do you think you made on the people you spoke to? And last but not least, did the body language (yours and theirs) match up with these impressions?

CHAPTER TWO
THE BODY LANGUAGE OF A BABY

"A crying baby is the best form of birth control." ~ Carole Tabron

If there was actually *much* truth to the quote under the title to this chapter, the world would be a whole lot less crowded, don't you agree? But there is probably at least a small bit of truth to it. Otherwise they still wouldn't be sending mechanical babies home from school with teenagers to care for over the weekend. You know what I'm talking about, right? The ones that are programmed to cry intermittently and don't stop unless you do just the right thing...but the 'right thing' isn't always the thing that worked the last time it cried?

Mechanical or not, those babies are pretty spot on when it comes to letting us know that they too, have the means to communicate. But unlike a real baby, the dolls don't have their own 'dialect' of body language. That's right—babies have a body language all their own. But if you are the parent, grandparent, sibling, or caregiver of a baby, you know how important it is for you to be able to understand what their hands, eyes, legs, head, and posture are saying.

The body language of a baby is something that develops and changes along with the rest of them. The more physically active they become and the more developed their cognitive and motor skills get, the more communicative their bodies get.

Birth to two months

The first movements a baby makes are purely reflex. Turning their mouth toward your cheek to 'kiss' you is nothing more than a reflex to root and latch on to the breast to eat. Grasping your finger and jerking in response to sudden or loud noises or a cold hand are also reflex movements. BUT... far be it from me to insinuate to any momma that every grin or smile from her baby those first few weeks is gas. No way am I going to go down that road because quite honestly, I don't think anyone knows for sure.

One thing I do know, however, is that those reflex movements become more intentional and meaningful in just a matter of a few short weeks after a baby makes its entrance into the world. By the time a baby is five or six weeks old their reflexes are taking a back seat to actual responses—some of which is body language.

Parents, especially moms, are quite good at reading their baby's body language. That in itself is somewhat instinctive, which when you think about it, is a bit of a paradox, considering the whole thing with baby's instincts being mistaken as body language early on.

The body language you need to be watching for and reading correctly in order to keep your baby (and everyone else in the house) happy and content is as follows:

- Knees and legs drawn up (usually accompanied by crying) indicates discomfort and pain.
- Stiffened legs, or legs and arms, indicates fear or pain (also often accompanied by crying).
- Rubbing their eyes indicates fatigue and sleepiness.

- Open arms that are relaxed indicate happiness and feeling safe and secure.
- Suddenly turning their head away from something or someone generally means they are overwhelmed or over stimulated.
- Smiling indicates happiness, security, and that they feel comfortable.
- Kicking their legs accompanied by fussing or crying indicates discomfort or frustration.
- Kicking their legs accompanied by smiles indicates excitement and happiness.
- An arched back indicates discomfort. It is their means of protest and attempted 'escape.'
- Sucking or chewing on their fist indicates hunger.

Three to eight months

As a baby grows they become more controlled in their movements. They can hold themselves upright without mimicking a bobble-head doll, even before they can sit by themselves without support or assistance. By the time they are midway through this three- to eight-month stage though, they become quite mobile, too. Rolling, scooting, and crawling to get everywhere and into everything is their main purpose in life. They become more vocal, as well, but they still communicate most of their thoughts and feelings via body language.

- Rubbing their eyes and yawning still denotes sleepiness and fatigue.
- Open arms now accompanied oftentimes with cooing and laughing indicates excitement and happiness.

- Reaching forward with open arms, along with lunging their whole body forward, is their way of saying they want to be held by whomever they are reaching for.
- Rubbing or pulling on their ears indicates discomfort and pain. The source is not always (or even usually) the ears. It can be from teething, gas, a sore throat, a stuffy nose, or even a headache that can accompany the stuffy nose problem.
- Babies this age still arch their backs in protest.
- Kicking their legs indicates they are bored and ready to move on to the next best thing. For example, a baby kicking their legs while sitting in their highchair is saying, "I want out of here!"

Nine months to one year

Babies in this age group are meeting and exceeding milestone after milestone when it comes to growth and development. One of those milestones is language, i.e., words and sounds. But make no mistake about it—body language is still a significant means of communication for these little ones. In fact, body language is often how we translate or decipher what all those sounds coming from their mouth actually mean.

For example, Emma points at the microwave and says 'dit don.' The translation: Emma wants the instant oatmeal her mom fixes for her in the microwave. On its own it would be impossible to figure out what 'dit don' means. And even if you tried, instant oatmeal would be the last...the *very last* thing you would think of. Right! But by using the body language of pointing, you can figure out that 'dit don' is her way of imitating the chime that indicates the microwave is done.

Knowing *that* is how the oatmeal is prepared makes perfect—or *nearly* perfect—sense.

The almost-one-year-old's body language 'vocabulary' is expanding at a rapid pace. By this age they…

- Reach for the person they want with wide-open, outstretched arms, and a great big smile.
- Stomp their foot and/or run away to signal resistance, rebellion, and attempted refusal to comply.
- Clap their hands in excitement.
- Rock back and forth from the waist while in a sitting position and with an upturned face to show excitement.
- Hide their face under their shoulder or hide behind someone they trust as a means of saying, "I'm shy," "I'm scared," or "I don't want to be noticed."
- Reach and grab to let you know that they want something.
- Hit at or push things away that they don't want or find threatening.
- Nod or shake their head to give a 'yes' or 'no' response.
- Clutch a favorite blanket, toy, or book close to their chest with an ironclad grip to indicate they need comfort and reassurance from fear, discomfort, pain, anxiety, or some other negative emotion or circumstance.
- Clench their fists, scowl, furrow their brows, keep their lips pressed tightly together, or squint their eyes to indicate they are in self-defense mode against

something that frustrates them or disrupts the orderliness of their world.
- Smile and frown to leave little to the imagination when it comes to deciphering their mood.
- Bite their lip, suck their thumb, twist their hair, chew on a toy or the hem of a blanket, rock back and forth from the heels or waist with their hands at their side to try to cope with their nervousness, fear, or reluctance to participate in a situation.

When it comes to interpreting the needs and wants of a baby, we are sometimes guilty of limiting our ability to communicate with the littles in our lives. We pride ourselves on being able to decipher their cries; recognizing the difference between a hungry cry, one that says, "I'm sleepy," and so forth. But if we will take the time and open our eyes (literally and figuratively speaking) we will be able to better meet their needs. And in the process, life will be a lot more pleasant and peaceful for everyone…which is always a plus.

When you think about it, it shouldn't really come as any great surprise to know babies use body language almost from the get-go. To help you see how true this is, I want to encourage you to do the following:

- Thumb through some photo albums containing snapshots of babies in your family. Pay special attention to their facial expressions and the way their bodies are positioned. Now compare these things to the obvious events, people, and surroundings in the pictures. Do they match up with what you just learned about a baby's body language?

- While sitting in church, a restaurant, or pushing your cart up and down the aisles of the grocery store, pay extra-close attention to the babies you see. Not in a way that will make the moms uncomfortable, of course, but as a casual observer. What do you notice about the way they are responding to their surroundings?
- Ask a few moms who have babies under one year of age how aware they are of their baby's body language. Give them a brief rundown of the things babies say with their bodies and ask these moms if they've noticed their baby 'speaking' baby body language.

CHAPTER THREE
THE BODY LANGUAGE OF A TODDLER

"Silence is golden unless you have a toddler in the house. Then it is suspicious." ~ Unknown

Few people would ever accuse their toddler of being too quiet or too dull. It's usually the other way around. Like the momma elephant in the book, "Five Minutes Peace," parents of toddlers enjoy the peace and quiet that comes after their toddlers are tucked in for the night or an afternoon nap. But at any other time, silence usually means T·R·O·U·B·L·E. Unless, of course, you've got a visual on them.

The body language of a toddler somewhat resembles that of a baby at times—especially when it comes to showing signs of nervousness, pain, and discomfort. Case in point: a nervous toddler bites their nails, twists their hair, sucks their thumb, or clutches a favorite toy or blanket in an effort to self-soothe. At other times, their body language is much more mature and 'telling.' In other words, a toddler leaves little doubt in anyone's mind when it comes to letting the world know what they want, what they think, and how they feel.

From their head to their toes, a toddler uses their body to express just about every emotion they are capable of feeling. So, if you have a toddler in your life, it would behoove you to have a working knowledge of what their bodies are telling you.

FYI: Your toddler will also be forever in your debt if you 'help' others read their body language, too. So, when Great Aunt Mable is coming full force toward your son, fingers ready to pinch his sweet, albeit chocolate-stained cheeks, don't apologize when he becomes wide-eyed and darts behind you clinging to your leg for dear life. And for the love of pizza, don't pull him out from behind you, making him 'fair game' for Mable. Instead, come to his defense. Tell Aunt Mable he's a bit shy and that he's not really all that into hugging, but he'll be happy to show her how well he can ride his new bike.

Reading your toddler's body language and responding accordingly makes for a happier, healthier, and more confident toddler. And in the process you and your home environment will be happier and healthier, too.

Head and face

- Ducking their head behind someone or something is a sign of shyness.
- Banging their head is a sign of frustration or anger.
- Dropping their head down (looking down) or turning away from you when you speak says, "I'm ashamed," "I don't want you to know what I'm doing (or what I've done)," or signifies guilt.
- A toddler who hides their head under their shirt, a blanket, or another similar object is scared, mad, sad, or trying to hide their guilt.
- When your toddler won't make eye contact they are scared, guilty, nervous, shy, or doing it out of rebellion.
- Squeezing their eyes shut is their way of trying to shut out something unpleasant—a memory or something going on they don't want to see. Eyes squeezed shut

- can also indicate physical pain or avoidance. They think if they can't see you, then you can't see them.
- Raised eyebrows and opening their eyes wide indicates surprise, shock, excitement, happiness, and awe.
- Furrowing or wrinkling their brows is a sign of confusion, uncertainty, disbelief, and worry.
- Blinking is a sign of nervousness and anxiety in most toddlers, but consistent and habitual blinking can be an indicator of a more serious condition such as autism or a neurological disorder.
- Lips clamped shut tightly are an indication of rebellion (you can't make me eat green beans no matter what!), anger, and/or to express their extreme dislike for something.

Arms and hands

- Rubbing their eyes is almost always a sign your little one is tired and sleepy. But not always. Sometimes it...
    o Indicates pain such as a headache or eye strain.
    o Is the result of allergies and the discomfort they can bring.
    o Is a physical means of 'rubbing out' an unpleasant sight or situation.
- Biting their nails, sucking their thumb, or twisting their hair around their finger indicates nervousness, stress, boredom, or serves as a means of self-soothing.
- Clapping shows excitement.
- Pushing *you* or another adult away with their hands is usually a sign they are seeking independence. "I can do it myself!" But just like rubbing their eyes can say different things, so can pushing someone away.

- o If they push someone away they know and trust, it is sometimes done to 'punish' that person for upsetting them or not giving them their way.
- o Pushing you or someone else they know away can also be their way of saying they want to be alone—that they want to self-soothe.
- o Sometimes your toddler will push you away because they don't want to comply with your requests or demands. It is an act of rebellion.
- o Pushing someone away they don't know well or trust (such as a distant relative or your college bestie) is usually their way of saying they don't trust that person, are intimidated or fearful of them, or (this is a good thing) that they understand what 'stranger danger' is and they are taking all those messages you've been sending to heart.
• Crossing their arms is a signal of defiance and rebellion.
• Crossing their arms may also signal that they are trying to defend themselves from hurtful words and actions.
• Hunched up shoulders are a sign your toddler feels intimidated, uncomfortable, and is intent on resisting whatever changes are being asked and expected of them.
• Clenched fists are signs of aggression, frustration, a readiness to fight (verbally or physically). Or, if accompanied by a smile, arched brows, and/or wide eyes, clenched fists can also indicate an attempt to contain their excitement.

- When your toddler walks nonchalantly and is subconsciously swinging their arms, they are telling you that all is right and good in their world. They are comfortable, secure, and happy.

Body and posture

- Slumped shoulders are a sign of sadness, submission, intimidation, or not feeling well.
- Hopping, jumping, dancing, and wiggling are indicators of joy, confidence, positive self-esteem, and feeling secure in their situation, surroundings, and in who they are. They are not afraid to express themselves or to be 'present and accounted for' in their social setting.
- Lying down and curling up in a fetal position can indicate several different things—both physically and emotionally.
    o Fear and anxiety
    o Fatigue
    o Pain
    o Embarrassment or shame
    o Lack of self-confidence
    o Trying to hide or remove themselves from a situation
- Outstretched arms are a sign of inclusion. They want you in their 'bubble space.' They need your comfort and support. They want to be held. They want to express their love for you.
- Eye contact is the same for a toddler as it is everyone else. Making eye contact with the person they are talking to or interacting with is a sign of self-

confidence, that they have nothing to hide, and that they trust in the other person. Eye contact is also a sign that the toddler is willfully engaged in the situation.

Legs and feet

- Tapping feet/toes can be an indicator of either nervousness or excitement. The difference will be evidenced by the other telling factors, which include a smile, scowl, loose comfortable posture, or clenched fists. Taking in the whole picture, so to speak, should tell you what your toddler is feeling.
- Stomping their feet indicates anger and frustration—usually because they aren't getting their way.
- Running away from you can signal their desire for independence (I can do it myself) or rebellion. Sometimes it is both at the same time.
- Running in general usually indicates excitement and says they are having fun.
- Limping indicates pain. The pain may be as simple as a growing pain (yes, it's a real thing), injury, a muscle cramp, or even something as simple to fix as their shoes being too small.
- Kicking—especially when paired with crying and/or flailing arms—is a sign of anger, resentment, rebellion, and defiance.
- Letting their legs go limp, as in not walking, might be a sign of tiredness and fatigue. It might even indicate illness or pain. More often than not, it is a sign of defiance and rebellion. Case in point...

Have you seen the 1993 version of the movie, *Dennis the Menace*? If you have, you probably know which scene I'm referring to. If not, you're about to. Either way, it's the perfect example of 'limp leg rebellion.'

Lea Thompson plays Dennis's mom, Alice Mitchell. She has just taken a job, putting her back in the workforce for the first time since having Dennis (played by Mason Gamble) five years ago. Alice arranges for another mom in the neighborhood to babysit Dennis while she is at work. But as it turns out, that mom just happens to be Margaret's mom. Margaret, as in the little girl who is Dennis's nemesis.

When they arrive at Margaret's house, Alice has to literally drag her son up the sidewalk because of his stubborn refusal to walk, aka 'limp leg rebellion.' To those of us watching the movie, it is comical, to say the least. But to Alice and any real-life mom who has been in her shoes (which I'm sure there have been many), comical is not the word they would use to describe the scene or the situation.

The body language of a toddler is not terribly difficult to read or translate. They are, for the most part, about as transparent as it gets. With a few exceptions here and there, they don't feel as if they have anything to hide, so they don't. To demonstrate this point, do the following:

- Play the 'face game' with a toddler or two by asking them to make a 'happy face,' a 'sad face,' a 'mean face,' a 'scared face,' a 'goofy or funny face,' and an 'angry face.' Notice how the rest of their body acts in conjunction with the face they make. In other words, notice how their posture changes, what they do with their arms and hands, and even how they position themselves.

- Observe a group of toddlers playing without any adult supervision (or at least none they are aware of). Take note of everything you can learn about the group by observing their body language. While doing so, decide the following: Who is shy? Who is happy? Who is the leader of the group? Who are the followers? Who would rather be playing something else? Who would rather be back with Mom or Dad?
- Ask a few moms of toddlers how accurate their toddler's body language is to what is actually happening with them. Ask them to give you a few examples.

CHAPTER FOUR
THE BODY LANGUAGE OF A CHILD

"The vivacity of children is always charming because it is always sincere." ~ Anonymous

Two-year-old Delia crouched down in the middle of the front yard with her arms and hands covering her head. This was her version of playing hide-n-seek with her mom and older siblings. It was cute. It was sweet. It was endearing. But fast-forward eight years to the day Delia's dad came home from work early and found ten-year-old Delia crouched between the trash cans in the pouring down rain. She'd been there for several hours. She had hidden herself there instead of getting on the school bus that morning. Her intention was to stay there until the bus came that afternoon. Her older siblings who were still living at home had driven themselves to school, so they didn't realize what she had done.

So what happened to Delia? What had changed in her life to change the meaning of her body language? In a word—TRAUMA. Delia had lost her mom and great-grandma in a tragic accident, leaving her too scared and paralyzed to live life. She was also too scared and confused to speak up about what she was feeling and thinking. But that day—a day Delia's dad says will be forever burned in his mind's eye—was the day Delia's dad started listening even more intently to his youngest daughter. Not just through her words, though, but through her body language as well.

School-age children (along with teenagers, as you will discover in the next chapter) are skilled in the art of saying something completely different than what they actually mean or want to say. For reasons we will discuss along the way, they are able to use their words to say what they think adults want them to say, but not really mean it. Sadly, it's not always their fault that they fall into this pattern of behavior. Unfortunately, some of the adults in their lives are guilty of pushing their children into a corner, so to speak, by putting unreasonable expectations on them. Sometimes adults are also guilty of setting an example of these behaviors.

Regardless of whether or not the body language of a school-age child is positive, negative, or somewhere in between, it is *always* important for us to read it, take heed of it, and act accordingly. If we do, everyone wins.

Head and face

- Nodding and shaking their head is an obvious sign of approval or non-approval.
- Tilting their head to one side usually indicates confusion, but with a desire to understand.
- Sometimes tilting their head to one side may indicate they are having difficulty hearing. This can be 'verified' by other actions including trying to clear their ear with a finger, or if they verbally ask you to repeat yourself.
- Smiles, frowns, and grimaces mean the same thing no matter how old we are.

- But a closed-lip smile almost always indicates that they are only pretending to be pleased or happy. This is one of those times when they are 'saying' what they believe you want to 'hear' (see).
- Furrowed brows indicate displeasure at times, but in most situations (especially in school) a furrowed brow is a sign of confusion and or concentration. They are trying to let a concept or idea sink in and make sense of it.
- Wide eyes and raised brows show excitement and surprise.
- Squinting can indicate the light is too bright (like it usually does in babies and toddlers), but at this age squinting their eyes is indicative of either physical pain, fearful anticipation, or feeling intimidated.
- Tugging on their ears is usually a sign of pain, which at this age will be paired with verbal confirmation.
- Rapid blinking is a sign of discomfort and/or stress.
- Darting their eyes back and forth is a clear indication they are hiding something and are being dishonest with you.
- Looking down at the ground when speaking is a sign of low self-esteem and feelings of inferiority.
- Looking around in different directions when talking to you versus making eye contact says the child is being dishonest and/or feels uncomfortable (nervous, intimidated, fearful). They are looking for the nearest exit (literally and figuratively speaking).
- Making eye contact is usually a sign of confidence, trust, and honesty. In a few rare instances, however,

standing straight and looking you in the eye can be an indication of fierce defiance.

- Making eye contact while you are talking also proves they are hearing AND listening to you.
- Pupil size is body language vocab, too. It isn't something we always take time to notice because it is such a deliberate gesture we don't want to be that obvious. Nevertheless, a dilated pupil indicates dishonesty, anxiety, and fear. Small/tiny pupils tell you that your child is telling the truth, that they are comfortable, and that they feel safe and secure.
- Puffing out their cheeks is one way your school age child demonstrates their resistance and hesitancy to respond to you in the way you desire or expect them to.
- Licking their lips is often more than the obvious, which is thirst. When your school age child licks their lips it is often a sign of anticipation. The anticipation can be either positive or negative (nervousness).
- Biting their lips is a sign of nervousness.
- When your child covers their mouth (other than when they are sneezing or coughing) they are trying to disguise their emotions or hide their inappropriate response.
- Thrusting the chin upward and outward is a sign of confidence. Sometimes, however, that confidence can be rebellious and defiant in nature. To determine which signal they are sending, you will need to read the rest of their body language (see body and posture section in this chapter) and translate the gleam in their eye. Is it glare-ish or is it sparkly?

Arms and hands

- Putting their hands up in front of their face palms out, is a sign of defense.
- Covering their face with their hands, palms facing in, is a sign of embarrassment or shame.
- Covering their face with their hands, palms facing in, can also be your school age child's way of hiding their true feelings.
- Drumming their hands on the table is your school age child's way of expressing boredom, nervousness, and impatience.
- Pushing you away with their hands might be a show of independence, depending on the accompanying body language. If, however, this action is combined with negative facial body language, or is forceful, it is most likely signaling anger and a refusal to comply.
- Shoving their hands in their pockets, drawing them up into their sleeves, or putting them behind their back is a sign of shyness and nervousness.
- Hugging themselves, which is a looser 'version' of crossing their arms over their chest, is a signal that your school age child is self-soothing and/or protecting themselves from emotional pain. It is saying, "I need to be listened to and loved."
- Nail biting, cracking/popping their knuckles, and twisting their hair are subconscious nervous habits that self-sooth and sometimes help the child think through or process thoughts and concepts.

- Rubbing the back of their neck is a sign that they are concentrating and trying to process thoughts and ideas.

Body and posture

- If your school age child pushes him/herself back from you (or anyone else) when they are hugged, they are saying they don't want to get too close (emotionally or physically).
- Moving backwards (even a step or two) while talking or being talked to indicates they need more personal space.
- Standing rigidly with their feet close together signals that they are in control of the situation. Or at the very least, they are in control of their actions and responses in the situation.
- Leaning into you when you are talking signifies trust, friendliness, and pleasure.
- Standing straight with their feet placed at shoulder distance says they have made up their mind about something. If their arms are crossed or their hands are locked behind their back, you should know you have little to no chance of getting them to change how they feel or think.
- Shoulders slumped and drawn in are a sign of timidity, shyness, and discomfort. They want to be somewhere...anywhere else.
- Shoulders slumped down, along with their chin dropped toward their chest is a sign of resignation and disappointment. They are conceding, but not happily.

- Lying down curled into a fetal position can be a sign that the child is in physical pain. This position can also indicate fear, grief, anxiety, and depression; or a desire to retreat and hide/escape from a situation. As is the case in other situations, you need to take a look at the big picture. What is going on around them? What has just happened, or is about to happen?

EXAMPLE: Are they grieving the loss of a beloved grandparent or pet? Are you and your spouse or ex-spouse fighting? Are they down for the count with the flu? Are they reliving the goal they scored earlier in the day…for the other team?

- Turning away from you while you are talking indicates boredom, disinterest, and sometimes defiance or rebellion. To determine which of these things is true you will need to take a look at the bigger picture. In other words, what are their eyes and posture telling you?
- Voluntary hugging, touching, and kisses on the cheek from your school age child are a welcome message to any parent. They tell you that your child feels loved, secure, and valued for who they are. Receiving these same gestures from you without resistance says the same thing.

FYI: Don't push your luck by insisting they hug or kiss you goodbye when their friends are around. They are trying to grow up, fit in, and prove to themselves, to you, and to their peers that they are independent. And also, FYI, that's not a bad thing. Independence for their child is (or should be) the goal of every parent.

Legs and feet

- Shuffling their feet is an indication that your child is uncomfortable, nervous, and looking for a way 'out.'
- Tapping their feet is also a sign of either nervousness or positive anticipation—the kind that says I can hardly wait my turn.
- Swaying back and forth from the waist or hips is a sign of being shy and wishing they weren't the center of attention.
- Stomping their foot or feet is an accentuation of trying to make a point, show displeasure for not getting their way, or expressing anger.
- Stepping or marching in place signals discomfort that might be physical or emotional, depending on the situation. It may be something as simple as needing to use the restroom but not sure if they should speak up. Or it could be something more along the lines of feeling extremely uncomfortable with the conversation or situation they are in. It is their way of wishing they could get away and preparing to do so.

If you have a school age child, or are around them very often, you know their verbal communication skills are well developed and their vocabulary is growing by leaps and bounds. But that doesn't mean they don't communicate with their bodies—because they do. What I'm saying is that by the time a child gets to be school age, their body language is somewhat of a 'second language' or what has been described by one mom as their 'two-part harmony.'

"I can't just listen with my ears," she said, "because if I did that I would miss a lot of important stuff. For example, if I took my twelve-year-old son's grumpy talk at face-value, I would discipline him unfairly. I say that because he is almost always easy to get along with. So, if he's got a case of the grumps or is argumentative, I take a closer look at what his body is saying. And without exception, I see/hear that something else is going on. Usually, he's just not feeling well."

That's a mom that is all-in when it comes to knowing what's going on with her kids. She's taking the time to hear both 'parts' (the harmony of verbal and body language) instead of hearing and responding incorrectly and inappropriately.

As parents, grandparents, and teachers, we automatically take the time to decipher a baby or toddler's body language because we know their verbal skills can't do much to convey the message they want and need to send. But once a child gets to be school age, we mistakenly assume that since their verbal skills are so advanced, body language no longer matters as much.

Big mistake! Just because children can talk doesn't mean they are able to communicate as effectively as they need to. Or more importantly, that they will have the confidence in themselves to do so! These little guys and gals are desperately trying to figure out who they are, how they fit into their peer groups, and who and what they need to be to please you. So, on behalf of all school age children out there, I am asking that you take the time to listen with your eyes as well as your ears.

Oh, and one more thing—you need to be sure that you are taking the time to make sure YOUR body language says what you need and want your children to hear.

- Watch one or two of the following movies with your school age children. As you watch, take note of the body language of the actors. Does it reflect what is happening? Also…take note of your child's body language during the movie—especially during scenes that portray strong positive or negative reactions and events. What do you notice about your child's body language? Does it reflect what is happening, i.e., are they empathizing with the movie's characters? Whose 'side' are they on?
    - "Diary of a Wimpy Kid"
    - "The Sandlot"
    - "Madeline" (not the animated version)
- Ask your child to tell you about a time when they were happy and excited, a time when they were sad, when they were scared, and when they felt shy. Notice the differences in their body language as they speak.
- Over the course of a weekend (or even longer) say as little to your child as possible. Instead, use their body language to determine what to say and how to say it.

EXAMPLES:

- "It looks to me like you are upset about what we are having for dinner, so let's make a deal. You eat tonight's dinner without complaining and tomorrow night I'll make your favorite."
- "I am sorry I embarrassed you by hugging you in front of your friends. I just love you so much. But I won't do it again if you don't want me to."

- "Stomping your foot because you're angry is not acceptable. But if you want to tell me why you are angry I will be glad to listen."
- "I saw the way you looked at the coach. Did she say something to hurt your feelings?"
- "You look scared. Please tell me why so we can talk about it."

CHAPTER FIVE
THE BODY LANGUAGE OF A TEENAGER

"It's difficult to decide whether growing pains are something teenagers have." ~ Unknown

When it comes to reading, listening to, and translating the body language of a teenager, the best and truest thing to be said is this: **Do it. Do it well. Do it always. Do it without apology.**

The teenage years are exciting, scary, fun, miserable, delightful, frightful, and full of choices and consequences. For everyone—both the teenager and his or her parents. But the teenage years are also something else—they are temporary.

Do you know what that temporary-ness means? It means that you only have a few years to get it right when it comes to reading your teenager's body language. Six short years. I know—in some ways those years seem like an eternity. Especially when you're in the thick of it and it's not the happy-happy-joy-joy event that *Brady Bunch* and *Leave it to Beaver* make it out to be. But ask any parent whose children are now grown, and they will tell you it flies by. They will also tell you not to waste these years.

They will tell you not to waste time:

- Assuming you know what your teenager is thinking

- Assuming that the words coming out of their mouths are the truth…the whole truth…and nothing but the truth
- Assuming that their silence means they have nothing to say
- Assuming that they don't want to talk to you
- Assuming that they don't want you to talk to them

Reading, understanding, and using your teenager's body language to effectively communicate with them on a level of intimacy, intellect, and respect that you both desire and need is essential for ~~good~~ great parenting. And don't think for one minute that cannot happen. YOU can be a fantastic parent to your teenager. No, really, you can. All it takes is lots of love, eyes that aren't jaded by presumptions and emotions, time, energy, and **knowing what your teen's body language is saying.**

So let's get started.

Head and face

- Tilting their head to one side indicates they are trying to understand what you are saying. They might also be deciding if they agree or disagree.
- The size of their pupils indicates whether or not they are being honest with you. Dilated (large) pupils are an indication of dishonesty.
- Rapid blinking is a sign of distress or nervousness.
- Scowls, smiles, frowns, and grimaces all tell you what your teen is thinking.

- Raised brows paired with a closed mouth (usually tight lips) says, "I'm shocked!" or "I can't believe that just happened!"
- Raised brows with an open mouth indicates surprise— usually one that is pleasant to them.
- A wrinkled brow and forehead are signs that they are trying to focus on what is being said.
- When a teenager squints their eyes at you, they doubt your sincerity and/or that you are being truthful with them.
- Dropping their head down to avoid making eye contact indicates shyness, regret, or admission of guilt.
- Turning their head away from you, looking from side to side, over their shoulder, or over your shoulder while you are talking indicates disinterest and boredom.
- Eye contact indicates interest and intentional listening. Eye contact also tells you that your teen isn't trying to lie to you or deceive you.
- Sucking their cheeks in tells you they are impatiently waiting to speak, but that they are having a hard time waiting their turn. It might also be an indicator that what they are about to say is going to be contrary to what you think or want to hear.
- Licking their lips signals positive anticipation.
- Biting the lower lip is a sign of negative anticipation.
- A tight-lipped smile is rarely sincere. More often than not it indicates a condescending attitude. They are not interested in what you have to say.

Arms and hands

- Using their hands to cover their mouth indicates they are trying to stifle or hide an inappropriate reaction (smile, etc.).
- Using their hand or hands to cover their mouth is also a sign that they are shocked, surprised, or scared.
- Using their hands to 'punctuate' what they are saying verbally indicates excitement or determination to establish their position of power.
- Wringing their hands together is a sign of frustration, anxiety, or deep concern/worry.
- Locking their hands behind their back says that they aren't going to concede their position or change their mind.
- Crossing their arms over their chest while standing tall with their feet together makes the statement that they are not backing down and that they are in control.
- Walking with their arms swinging loosely by their sides is a sign that they are comfortable, at ease, secure, and happy with the way life is going.
- Using their arms and hands to push you away signals that they don't want you in their personal space.
- If you move toward them and they position their arms firmly at their sides, put them behind their back, or pick something up, they are saying they do not want to be hugged or touched. They would prefer that you keep your distance.
- If you move toward them and they lean forward a bit, open their arms (even partially), or extend one or both

arms, they are saying they will reciprocate a hug, handshake, fist bump, or other similar greeting.
- Biting their nails, cracking/popping their knuckles, or twisting their hair are all signs of nervousness. They are subconscious acts, though, so they don't even realize they are telling on themselves.
- Hugging themselves is a means of self-soothing and protection from physical and emotional pain.
- Shrugging their shoulders indicates an attitude of indifference and disinterest.

Body and posture

- Turning away from you when you speak to them is a sign of defiance, distrust, or disinterest. The specifics of the situation will tell you which it is.
- Leaning into you or away from you when you talk indicates their level of comfort, trust, and affinity toward you.
- Sitting with their legs turned toward you indicates attentiveness, trust, and interest in what you have to say.
- Reclining back on their elbows with their legs stretched out in front of them tells you your teen is relaxed, comfortable, and feels safe, secure, and confident.
- Standing with their shoulders back and their chest out says they are confident, sure of their position, and in control of their thoughts and feelings.
- Sitting with their legs crossed signals that they want privacy or that they are unwilling to share their feelings. The reason may be something as simple as not

being in the mood, to not trusting you to take them seriously.
- Twisting from the waist while talking or listening is a sign of being shy, insecure, or in a hurry to move on.
- When your teenager leans into you from a standing or sitting position, with their arms planted firmly at their sides they are exerting their independence. They are letting you know they feel confident and in control of the situation. There could possibly be an element of rebellion involved, depending on the situation.
- Fidgeting while sitting or standing is a sign that your teenager is uncomfortable. Their discomfort usually comes from the fact that they are being dishonest with you and are afraid of being 'found out' or because they are being disciplined. Their discomfort might also stem from being shy and feeling anxious about being the center of attention, being put on the spot, or merely being out of their comfort zone.
- Sitting in a slumped position is fairly common among teenagers. It usually means they are at ease and comfortable with their surroundings, relaxed and confident they can deal with whatever is going on around them.
- Standing in a slumped or slouchy position is also a sign that your teenager is relaxed and confident. The exception to this and to sitting in a slumped position is if they have their chin tucked into their chest, keeping their head down, and not making eye contact. If this is the case, they are intimidated, feel ashamed, and beaten down.

- When your teenager is curled up in a fetal position they are either sick, frightened, or depressed. NOTE: When a teenager's response to something is to assume the fetal position, parents (or supervising adults) need to take it seriously. They don't do this without a legitimate reason. It is a cry for help that needs to be answered.

Legs and feet

- Stepping in place from one foot to another indicates boredom, being ill at ease, and impatience. This might stem from shyness, their lack of honesty, or disinterest in what is going on.
- Tapping their foot slowly indicates they are thinking about what is being said or planning their next move.
- Tapping their foot quickly is a sign of impatience.
- Repeatedly rising up on their tiptoes and then falling back on flat feet is a sign that your teenager is trying to do better. Reach higher (figuratively speaking).
- Shuffling their feet is a sign a teenager is ill at ease. They may be shy, afraid of being 'found out,' or bored. They are subconsciously trying to 'escape.'
- Standing rigidly indicates either anger or fear. The specifics of the situation along with other body language will tell you which it is.
- Rocking back and forth on their heels is a sign of boredom. They can't wait to get away.
- Standing or sitting with their knees turned in and pressed together says they are not going to let you invade their privacy. They are trying to protect their personal space.

Personal space and privacy are highly valued and coveted by teenagers. And because you love and respect your teenagers, you need to give them these things. Within reason.

While body language is important at every age and stage in life, the teenage years are arguably the most important when it comes to reading body language and reading it in harmony with their verbal language. FYI: It is also essential that you read the entire body, so to speak. For example, a hand movement or position can mean more than one thing depending on facial expressions.

If you doubt the validity of what I just said you need to take a minute or two to let the following statistics from the American Psychological Association sink in:

- 59% of teenagers say that trying to balance their schedules and activities is highly stressful.
- 40% of teenagers say they neglect responsibilities because of the stress they experience due to expectations placed on them.
- 40% of teenagers say they are irritable due to stress when they really don't want to be.

Source: Teen Stress and Anxiety: Facts and Statistics (evolvetreatment.com)

Additionally, several medical journals have released studies that show the following to be true of teenagers:

- Over 10% of all teenage girls have an eating disorder.
- Nearly half of all teens (boys and girls) are bullied (made fun of) because of their weight (overweight).

- Over 15% of teenagers *seriously* consider suicide, with 8% of them attempting to take their own life more than once.
- 2% of teenagers admit to having a phobia that prevents them from doing something their peers do.

The reason I want to draw your attention to these things is to drive home the point of how vital it is to their wellbeing that you are able to read their body language. Think about it—your teenagers aren't going to come to you and say things like, "I hate my body so I'm going to starve myself." Or "I can't deal with the pressure. I just want to die." Or "I decided I was done with just saying 'no', so I started using meth and now I'm hooked."

No, it's up to you and to anyone and everyone who cares about a teenager to be vigilant without being paranoid, watchful without being nosy, and informed without being intrusive. The good news is that you can do all three successfully when you take the time to know and read their body language. And for the record, it can, and often does, make the difference between life and death.

I realize that last statement might sound a bit ominous and overly dramatic, but it's not. It's the reality of the world we live in. So keeping that and the old saying, "Better safe than sorry" in mind, here are some tips and suggestions you need to follow:

- Spend time observing your teenager in a variety of situations: sporting events, extra-curricular events, with their friends, at home, in a more formal setting like at church, a restaurant, school assembly, or as a spectator at an event. What do you notice about them?

Does their body speak similarly in most or all situations? Do they seem to be more comfortable at one time over another? Do they ever appear fearful or intimidated? Take heed of what you notice and act accordingly.
- Spend some time every day... every single day talking *to* your teenager. Not talking *at* them but talking *to* them. Listen to what they say. Watch what they are saying. Watch how they respond to you. What do you hear? What do you see?
- Take the time to make sure *your* body language is sending the messages you want your teens to receive.
- In addition to observing your teenager's body language, you will also need to use your powers of observation for picking up on things like:
    o Changes in their friends—the ones they spend time with.
    o A drop in their grades.
    o Dropping out of extra-curricular activities they formerly enjoyed.
    o Mood swings.
    o Spending a lot more time alone.
    o A change in their style of dress, their taste in music, and their attitude toward you and other family members.
    o Talking about death—usually glamourizing it.
    o No longer talking about the future.
    o Wearing baggy clothes and/or long sleeves even in hot weather.
    o Using the restroom immediately after eating.
- Act accordingly to what you learn from the above.

- Let your teenager know it is okay to cut a few things from their schedule, so they'll have time to do absolutely nothing.
- Make sure your teenager knows it is more than okay to be confused, to not have their future mapped out, and to not be a clone to what society considers normal or desirable.

CHAPTER SIX
BODY LANGUAGE IN LOVE AND MARRIAGE

To find someone who will love you for no reason, and to shower that person with reasons, that is the ultimate happiness. ~ Robert Brault

As I thought about how to begin this chapter, my mind kept going back to couples I know who have been married a long time. A *very* long time...as in sixty 'plus' years. And in thinking about these couples, I thought about their responses to the question they had been asked on numerous occasions. You know which one I'm talking about, don't you? It's the question, "What is your secret to a long and happy marriage?"

Most of the answers they gave, that I will list below, will probably not come as any surprise to you. But here's something you probably haven't noticed before—most of their answers have more to do with what they *do* than what they *say*. Don't get me wrong—verbal communication is essential for a happy, healthy relationship, but being able to read each other's mood and pick up on each other's signals is every bit as important.

If you aren't convinced this is true, take a look at the list of tips and suggestions couples gave for their long, loving, and fulfilling marriage:

- Know your spouse's 'love language' so you can hear it and speak it.
- Be yourself.
- Just. Be. Nice.
- Communication. Communication. Communication.
- Don't be afraid or too proud to be wrong.
- Remember to notice the little things.
- Don't assume. When in doubt, ask.
- Hear with your eyes because it's not always what they say, but how they say it.
- Touch each other. Holding hands, hugging, kissing, and a reassuring hand on the back, arm or shoulder are powerful expressions of love. They also connect you two in a way that you aren't connected to anyone else.
- Take the time to learn how to read each other because sometimes *saying* nothing at all is the best way to get to the heart of the matter.

(**Source**: couples married forty, fifty, sixty, and sixty-three years.)

Head and face

- A slight nod is a word of approval—especially if it is accompanied by a smile.
- Laying their head on your shoulder is their way of saying they need comfort and to rest in their safe place.
- Looking away or from side to side when you are talking is a sure sign that they are not paying attention to what you are saying.
- Frowns, smiles, and scowls mean the same thing in a marriage as they do in any other relationship.

- Biting their lip while you are talking signals that they are waiting their turn to speak. It can also be a sign that that they are worried about the way the conversation is going or the subject matter.
- Licking their lips means your spouse is waiting to jump into the conversation. Whether they want to agree or argue with you will be evident by other body language.
- Raising their brows and opening their eyes wider while talking or being spoken to is an indication that they are either excited or shocked.
- Moving their head toward you, putting it out in front of the rest of their body, is like putting an exclamation point at the end of their statement. They want you to know they mean business.
- Furrowed brows indicate frustration, confusion, and irritability.
- Shaking their head slowly is a sign of disapproval and disagreement.
- Shaking their head vigorously is a signal they want you to stop speaking and that they are not in agreement with you.
- A closed-lip smile (smirk) is a sure sign of disapproval and disgust.
- Tucking their head to their chin or tilting it down and to the side is an act of submission due to intimidation.
- Squinted eyes say they are trying to understand but growing weary of doing so.
- When your spouse closes their eyes while you are speaking to them, you need to observe the rest of their body language and subject matter. The combination of these three things will tell you if they are trying to shut

you out (ignore you), wishing the conversation away because it is too painful, envisioning what you are saying, relaxing or letting the emotional warmth and security they feel wash over them.

- Darting their eyes in different directions versus making eye contact with you while speaking is an indication that your spouse is uncomfortable. Possible reasons for their discomfort include their lack of trust in you, feeling intimidated or fearful of you, wishing to avoid the subject of the conversation, or they are being dishonest with you.
- Eye contact with eyes open to a normal size or slightly larger indicates you have their full and undivided attention, love, and respect.
- Eye contact with one or both brows slightly arched, and a slight smile indicates they want to be alone and more intimate with you.
- Rolling their eyes while you are talking indicates they are bored or that they don't believe you.
- A playful kiss on the lips or cheek is an act of encouragement or just a reminder that you are loved.
- A deeper kiss or one that is paired with another form of contact says they want to be intimate with you.

Arms and hands

- Wringing their hands is a sign of worry and fretful anticipation of what you have to say or how you will react to what they tell you.
- Flexing their fingers while opening/shutting their hands is a sign that they are preparing for an argument or confrontation.

- Clenched fists indicate anger, fear, or anticipation (positive or negative). You need to read the other signals their body is sending to determine the true meaning.
- Biting their nails, cracking/popping their knuckles, subconscious finger tapping, and twirling their hair are all signs of nervousness.
- Rubbing the back of their neck is an indication of tension. They are trying to rub it away.
- Scratching their head is a sign of confusion and that they are trying to make a decision.
- Placing their hand on their forehead is a sign they are stressed.
- Covering their mouth with their hand is a show of surprise, shock, or fear.
- Covering their hand with their mouth while talking to you is their way of trying to 'soften the blow,' i.e., make their words less harsh, or put a buffer between them and you.
- Pressing their hand to their mouth with their fingers pointing up toward their nose is a sign that they are trying to repress their thoughts and inclination to speak out.
- Crossing their arms at the chest and holding on to their elbows is a sign of defiance. They are ready to argue and hold their ground.
- Hugging themselves while talking or listening indicates they don't feel safe with you, respected by you, or loved by you.

- Pointing their hand or hands toward you with their palms faced out indicates they are setting boundaries in place that they don't want you to cross.
- Pointing their hand or hands out toward you as if they are getting ready to clap indicates they are making a point. They need you to understand where they are coming from.
- Stretching their arms above their head and/or arching them behind their back usually indicates boredom and inattentiveness. If, however, it is paired with a soft smile, you can take it as a sign of being relaxed and taking comfort in what is being said and/or done.
- Placing their arms stiffly at their side while speaking or listening means they are not going to give in on how they think/feel about a matter.
- Rubbing your hand, arm, leg, shoulder, or back with their hand is a sign they are craving more intimacy with you.
- A gentle squeeze of the hand or even just simply holding hands is a statement that says they are glad you two belong together.
- Hugging is a sign of acceptance, forgiveness, a need for comfort, or a desire for intimacy.
- Rubbing their temples while talking or listening to you says they are frustrated, irritable, and don't want to hear what you have to say.
- Rubbing their palms together in an up and down motion indicates they are contemplating what you said and the response they want to make.

- When your spouse links their arm through yours, they are telling you they trust you to take care of them—physically and emotionally.

Body and posture

- Leaning into you while sitting, standing, or lying down indicates they feel safe, loved, and respected. They also want to offer you the same.
- Leaning forward from the waist while standing and talking to you is a sign your spouse wants to make a point.
- Sitting with their legs 'falling open' is an invitation to speak freely with them.
- Crossed legs or legs turned to one side says they are listening out of obligation.
- Slumped shoulders and chin tucked toward the chest is a sign they need comfort and encouragement.
- A rigid posture indicates anger or fear.
- Rocking back and forth on their heels while in a conversation with you indicates boredom.
- Fidgeting (not being able to stand or sit still) while with you signals one of the following: intimidation, boredom, or that they are being dishonest with you.
- Turning to the side and looking in various directions while talking or listening to you is a sign they want to escape. They are either bored, anxious, fearful, or feeling guilty.
- Sitting with their back to you (even partially) indicates they are not interested in what you have to say. Either they don't trust you, or they disagree and are not interested in changing their mind.

- Curling up in a fetal position indicates your spouse is either fearful of you or no longer trusts you enough to let you into their heart and mind to know their thoughts and feelings.
- If your spouse leans toward you while sitting down, they want you to know they are ready to listen and that they either agree with you or are willing to compromise.
- Snuggling up close to you during conversation or while just hanging out is a reminder that they love you and are thankful and happy to be able to share life with you.
- Sprawling out in a relaxed manner on the bed, couch, or floor tells you your spouse is open to what you have to say. They feel comfortable and in sync with you.

Legs and feet

- Tapping their foot rapidly while talking and/or listening to you is a sign of boredom or frustration.
- Pacing while talking or listening shows anxiety and the need to speak.
- Playing 'footsie' (yes, it's a real thing) is a request for intimacy.
- Shuffling one or both feet while talking or listening is usually a sign of boredom. It might also be a subconscious admission of guilt, too, depending on the circumstances.
- Stretching their legs and feet out toward you while sitting or lying down is an indication of trust and intimacy.

If you are married, how often did you nod your head in agreement or think to yourself, "So *that's* why he/she does that!" Body language is powerful. Don't you agree?

To prove my point let's take a look at a few examples. Some are real-life while others are theatrical. No matter what the source, though, they drive home the truth that the level of intimacy between married couples is heightened tremendously when they take the time to read, translate, and appreciate each other's body language.

"I can still remember how I could feel her shoulder shaking under my hand when she finally took a big, deep breath and slid her finger underneath the edge of the envelope. But it wasn't until after she actually read the words printed on that telegram that the tears came—both hers and mine."

"Somehow I managed to go ahead and do my chores. Mom probably insisted—thinking the distraction would help pass the time until Dad came home. As I milked and fed the cow and gathered the eggs, I remember feeling like it wasn't real and that when Dad got home everything would be ok. It wasn't."

"Dad was a feed and tobacco salesman and spent a lot of time driving from store to store servicing his customers. The stores he went to were scattered around the little communities in Miller and Pulaski counties in Missouri where I grew up. There was no way to get a hold of him so he could come home early. We just had to wait. Thinking about it just now, I feel so sorry for Mom. I wonder how many times she went over and over in her mind just how she would tell Dad about the telegram—or if she even would. Maybe she would just hand it to him."

"As it turned out she didn't have to do either. He could tell the minute he walked through the door that we had received a piece of paper that turned my family's life upside down."

(Excerpt from "All My Love, George…Letters From A WWII Hero" by D Noble; 3rd edition 2020)

A husband and wife can know what is in each other's hearts by the look on their faces.

In the movie, *Father of The Bride—Part Two*, George (played by Steve Martin) doesn't do a very good job of supporting his wife Nina (played by Diane Keeton) when the couple finds out they are expecting a baby. Now mind you, just days earlier their daughter and son in-law announced they were having their first child, which meant George and Nina were going to be grandparents for the first time.

Anyway, the shock proves to be too much for George, which leaves Nina to process the news on her own. So, when George tries to make up for his lack of husbandly support by cracking a joke, Nina puts up her hand, and turns and walks away; leaving George to find his own way home.

George knew better than to try to follow Nina or convince her to not leave him 'stranded.' He would have no trouble getting home, but he knew Nina needed to have some time to calm down before he did. For that matter, he needed time to get himself together so he could be supportive of his wife.

David and Eleanor are another example—a real life example, as in they are actual people. Not actors on a stage or in front of a screen.

David and Eleanor were childhood sweethearts who married just days (ten to be exact) before David was deployed overseas for a year. More than a few people questioned the wisdom of Eleanor's parents for giving the young people their blessing for the kids to get married, but they knew in their hearts they were doing the right thing.

Fast-forward almost a year later when the newlyweds were finally reunited. Both Eleanor and David admitted to feeling nervous about the homecoming. They didn't doubt their love for each other, but a lot had happened to David while he was overseas. How deeply had it affected him? Would it change the way he treated Eleanor? His personality? His sense of humor?

One only had to see the look on both of their faces, the way they clung to one another, and the way they sort of just melted together to know that the words they'd written in their letters were far more than just words.

Body language is the most telling sign of sincerity and genuineness in a marriage. The body speaks far more eloquently AND truthfully than words ever can or ever will.

Margaret was so sick and weak she could barely speak. The oxygen mask she wore also made talking all but impossible. But the agony in her eyes, the tears that trickled down her face, and the way she flinched and twitched told Ralph, her husband of sixty-six years, that his beloved wife and best friend was in extreme pain.

He mentioned it to every nurse and aide that came into her room, but none of them took him seriously. Or rather, they thought he was being over-solicitous and a worry wart. But when he refused to dismiss what he knew was his wife's pleas for help and relief, one of the nurses finally took the time to thoroughly evaluate the situation. And not to Ralph's surprise, they found that Margaret's IV had burst through a vein and the potassium was running under her skin, making her feel as if her skin was on fire.

The nurses felt horrible about the oversight and did everything they could as quickly as possible to bring relief to their patient. They also were profusely apologetic to Ralph for not believing him. He graciously accepted their apologies but told them he hoped that in the future they would be more respectful of the relationship between a husband and wife and their ability to read each other's looks and movements.

Couples—especially those who have been married as long as Ralph and Margaret—are able to read each other's needs and concerns through body language.

Trevor and Nina, on the other hand, had a long-distance romance and a long-distance marriage the first three years they were husband and wife. The lack of living together on a daily basis made it difficult for the couple to get to know each other. The time they *did* spend together those first few years they spent being on their 'best behavior.' They were never together for any length of time to be able to read each other's body language. So, when the two finally started living together full time their marriage took a nosedive.

Nina accused Trevor of being inconsiderate and disrespectful. Trevor was convinced Nina had turned into the most selfish person on earth. They contemplated returning to their former living arrangement since it seemed to work so well, but when a trusted friend suggested that it was their original living arrangement that caused their problems, they decided to seek counseling.

Two years later they saw their counselor for the last time. At their last meeting, Trevor joked that they were so good at reading each other's body language he didn't even have to ask Nina when she wanted a foot rub or snack during the last few weeks she was pregnant with their first child.

"I just knew," he smiled. "I could tell by the look in her eyes and the way she licked her lips while looking toward the kitchen."

"I have to admit he's right," Nina laughed. "I don't think I ever asked out loud even once."

Couples who read each other best spend time just being together; getting to know each other's whims, ways, and wishes.

- Talk to two or three couples who have been married several years. Ask them how often they rely on body language to know what each other wants.
- Make a conscious effort to read your spouse's body language. If you are in doubt, ask them if you are reading them correctly.
- Take the time to think about your own body language. Do your movements, posture, and expressions convey the love and affection you have for your spouse? Would they have reason to doubt your commitment to your marriage, or can they rest assured your love is truly "…until death do us part"?

CHAPTER SEVEN
BODY LANGUAGE BETWEEN FRIENDS...OR ARE THEY FOES?

"The best kind of friend is the one you could sit on a porch with, never saying a word, and walk away feeling like that was the best conversation you've had." ~ Unknown

If you were to do a search for the best movies, books, and television shows about friends, the lists you'd find would consist of titles going back as far as the level of trust between Lewis and Clark, the kinship of Tom Sawyer and Huck Finn, Anne of Green Gables and Diana, and Nancy Drew and her pals Bess Marvin and George Fayne. Then as you worked your way up the list you would undoubtedly find Lucy and Ethel, Johnny Carson and Ed McMahon, the Golden Girls, and the infamous half-dozen, aka Chandler, Joey, Ross, Phoebe, Monica, and Rachel.

Each and every one of these friendships surely had its ups and downs. In reading about their lives and the adventures they shared, you will see that there were times when they could 'read each other like a book' and then there were times when they couldn't. Several of these friendships proved beyond a shadow of a doubt that opposites really do attract, while others prove that the relationship worked as well as it did only because they were able to read each other so well.

In each of the previous chapters, we have dissected the different areas of the body and how they speak to us throughout the various ages and stages of our life. From infancy to adulthood we have seen how we use our body—consciously or otherwise—to let people know what we are thinking, how we feel, and even how we perceive ourselves.

So, by now you know that...

- Shuffling feet are a sign of boredom.
- A lack of eye contact indicates dishonesty, deception, intimidation, and other types and reasons for avoidance.
- Leaning in with the body or turning toward someone is an indication of trust, genuine interest, and intimacy.

You also know how to read facial expressions (frowns, smiles, furrowed brows, grimaces, raised brows, and scowls) that allow you to discern how your friends feel and think. Consequently, instead of going back over all of these signals again, we are going to start learning how to put them to use. Why? Because knowledge without practical application isn't worth much. Think about it—what good is a skilled surgeon if they refuse to step foot into the operating room?

The same is true when it comes to body language. It does absolutely no good to know it but not use it. Equally true, you need to make sure you know how to read it properly. Remember: Not using body language or not using it *properly* can cause irreparable damage to relationships. It might also cause you to miss out on a relationship that has the potential to bring life-long fulfillment, joy, and satisfaction.

Keeping these things in mind, let's spend some time looking at how to respond to body language in a variety of situations and circumstances. We won't cover everything. It would be unrealistic to presume we could. Hopefully, though, you will be able to take something from what we *do* cover to apply to your relationships; using them to speak and translate your own unique body language dialect.

Head and face

Have you ever seen the movie, *Gone With the Wind*? Silly question (I hope). It is an infamous classic. There could never be another like it…or even close to it. So many of its scenes and lines are embedded in our minds because…well, just because. Included in these forever-in-our-mind images are a) the one of Scarlett O'Hara Butler's eyes seething with anger and when she realizes Rhett has been right all along—Ashley Wilkes never did love her like he loved his sweet wife, Melanie, and b) the grit and determination she had to get home to Tara despite the rampages of war going on all around her (literally).

The point I want to make is that Scarlett could have said anything. But there wouldn't have been enough oxygen on earth for her to say anything that would have changed the truth—the truth her eyes ~~spoke~~ shouted loud and clear for all to see. Why? Because the body language spoken by our head and face is both convincing and convicting.

- Tilting the head to one side indicates someone is trying to understand what you are saying. They might also be deciding if they agree or disagree.
    - In a friendship, romantic relationship/marriage, or even a parent/child

relationship, you will need to decide how detrimental it is that the person you are speaking to understands and/or agrees with you. This is often referred to as 'picking your battles.' Often times it is best to agree to disagree.

- o If you are teaching a concept or lesson, this body language indicates you need to stop to give the person time to process or ask questions. You might also need to take a different approach to your presentation (depending on the person's learning style or personality type).

- o If YOU are the one scratching your head and no one responds appropriately, stop and speak up.

- The size of someone's pupils indicates whether or not they are being honest with you. Dilated (large) pupils are an indication of dishonesty. Restricted (small) pupils indicate they are being truthful.

  - o This is not an easy one to discern because it usually requires you to be 'up close and personal' to the point of invading their personal space. Therefore, you usually have to read the other signals they are sending and use them to decide if you need to pay close attention to the size of their pupils.

  - o If someone's body language says they are lying to you, you have every right to call them on it, but how you do it determines a) how successful you will be and b) the outcome and how the outcome affects your relationship.

- The best way to hold someone accountable for lying to you is to give them the opportunity to come clean, so to speak, without making them feel ashamed and undeserving of your friendship and/or love. There are a number of ways to do this.

    - Use YOUR body language (eye contact, turn toward them, smile, and gently nod while they are speaking) to let them know you want to continue the relationship, but that it is not acceptable to lie.

    - Use your body language to let them know that YOU know they are being dishonest (don't break eye contact, do stand or sit up straight, lean forward a bit from the waist, stay calm, and listen); make sure your facial expressions show your skepticism in their 'story.'

    - When you express your verbal doubts about what someone is telling you, be sure you extend your hands toward them with the palms facing up to let them know you are willing to give them a chance to 'fess up.'

- When someone lies to you it is only natural that your trust in them is fractured or broken. The intimacy of the relationship, the length of the relationship, the nature of the relationship, and the lie itself usually determines how, how long, or even if your trust in that person can be repaired and restored. This is something you have to decide for yourself, but the person's body language can help determine whether or not you feel the relationship is worth the risk. A handshake, a pat on the back, a hug, or a kiss (depending on the nature of the relationship) are acceptable ways to assure someone that the relationship can weather a lie.
- Hand gestures and/or a firm nod of the head and raised brows are body language that should accompany verbal confirmation that you are willing to work with them to reestablish your trust in them, but that it is contingent on their total honesty from that moment on.

- Rapid blinking is a sign of distress or nervousness.
  - When someone is nervous in your presence you need to reassure them. You can do this with your body language, or with a combination of words and body language. Laying a hand on their shoulder, taking their hand in yours, smiling, leaning toward them during the conversation, giving slight nods of approval, and inviting them to make

themselves physically comfortable in your presence are all ways to alleviate someone's nervousness.

- o If you are the one who is nervous, taking slow, deep breaths, standing up straight and tall, and maintaining eye contact no matter what, will increase your level of confidence.

- o Remembering that no one can intimidate you without your permission (consciously or subconsciously), speak and listen while holding your eyes open just a bit wider than normal to help prevent you from blinking. If the conversation or events make you feel uncomfortable and/or unsafe and disrespected, turn and leave.

- Raised brows paired with a closed mouth (usually tight lips) says, "I'm shocked!" or "I can't believe that just happened!"

  - o If the surprise or shock is positive in nature, congratulate the person, share in their excitement, and encourage them to believe the news and enjoy it. You can express yourself verbally and/or use body language that includes a high-five, hug, pat on the back, smiles, and nods of approval.

  - o If the surprise or shock is negative, sad, or disturbing in nature, offer comfort by way of a gentle touch, empathetic and sympathetic smiles and nods, a hug, holding their hand securely in yours, or by sitting close by and just being silent with them.

- When someone drops their head down to avoid making eye contact it indicates shyness, regret, or admission of guilt.
    - o We should never want to intimidate anyone or make them feel uncomfortable around us. This never does anything positive for the relationship, no matter what that relationship is (work, friendship, romantic, parent/child, etc.). Therefore, the best way to respond to body language of this nature is to put the person at ease. You can do this by smiling, making eye contact, positioning yourself to their level (sit if they are sitting, stoop to their height, etc.), facing them while either of you is speaking, offering a reassuring nod, taking their hands in yours (if appropriate), and offering them words of assurance and comfort.

- Turning their head away from you, looking from side to side, over their shoulder, or over your shoulder while you are talking indicates disinterest and boredom.
    - o Keep things short, sweet, and to the point. Don't belabor the conversation. Don't over-analyze or micromanage the situation.

- Don't make someone feel guilty or 'less' for not being all-in or as interested as you are in something.

- As an employer, teacher, or someone pursuing a friendship or romantic relationship, you can take this as a sign that this person is not a good fit for the job or is not going to reciprocate your attentions and affections, so move on.

• Sucking their cheeks in tells you they are impatiently waiting to speak, but that they are having a hard time waiting their turn. It might also be an indicator that what they are about to say is going to be contrary to what you think or want to hear.

- State your case and invite them to speak. Make sure, however, that your invitation is sincere and that you respect their opinions and viewpoints—even if they differ from yours.

- Listen intently by maintaining eye contact, sitting or standing still with your body positioned toward them, and without shuffling your feet, crossing your arms and/or legs, and by making sure your facial expressions don't shut them down and give them the impression that you are dismissing them as unimportant or wrong.

• A tight-lipped smile is rarely sincere. More often than not it indicates a condescending attitude. They are not interested in what you have to say.

- If the person (particularly your child, spouse, or employee) needs to hear what you have to say, you need to meet their body language resistance with firm, but gentle reminders that you are in control and that they need to respect your authority. You can do this using verbal communication along with a calm, relaxed, yet confident posture; consistent eye contact; speaking with your hands in your lap or out in front of you (palms up or down, but not with clenched fists); facing the person straight-forward; and keeping your chin erect and straight, or possibly tilted upward a bit.

- If the conversation and/or interaction is non-essential, let it go. There is enough negativity in the world without submitting yourself or someone else to that which is unnecessary.

- Before moving on and out of the relationship, though, you might consider asking the person why they feel the way they do and what, if anything, can be done to rectify the situation. If the problem can be fixed by doing something as simple as changing an assignment or expectations, or agreeing to disagree, then so be it.

Arms and hands

Sheldon Cooper's obligatory, "There, there," accompanied by an oh-so-awkward pat on the shoulder is proof that not everyone is fluent in body language. But don't think for a moment that Sheldon doesn't speak body language. In fact, that awkward pat on the shoulder is his way of shouting, "I am not capable of or comfortable with intimacy!"

FYI: If you don't know who Sheldon Cooper is, watch an episode (or the entire series) of *The Big Bang Theory*.

Using our arms and hands to convey our thoughts and feelings is as natural to us as breathing. If you don't believe that, try going an entire day without using your hands or arms when you speak.

Keeping that in mind, take a few minutes to familiarize yourself with what people are saying to you, and vice versa, through the body language of the arms and hands.

- Using their hands to cover their mouth indicates they are trying to stifle or hide an inappropriate reaction (smile, etc.).
    - Who among us hasn't done this? We all have…and will continue to do so. If it is a child, you might want to consider complimenting them and/or thanking them for stifling their reaction instead of being rude and/or inappropriate.
    - If someone does this in response to something you say or do, reassure them that it is okay to be honest about how they feel and what they think.
- Wringing their hands together is a sign of frustration, anxiety or deep concern/worry.
    - Offer your assistance, advice, comfort, and encouragement.

- o   If you are the cause of their angst, apologize (if appropriate) and/or do what you can to alleviate the problem.
- Crossing their arms over their chest while standing tall with their feet together makes the statement that they are not backing down and that they are in control.
  - o   The first thing you need to do in this instance is decide if the 'battle' is worth fighting. In other words, if the person is taking a stand and has no intention of compromising or changing their mind, then move on.
  - o   The exception to the above statement is if you are dealing with your children, students or someone over whom you have authority. EXAMPLE: A law enforcement officer facing someone resisting arrest or a referee against a coach or player.
  - o   If you decide to pursue the issue, you need to remain calm and even-tempered. It will also be to the advantage of everyone involved if you counterbalance their body language with some of your own. Make sure your arms aren't crossed to signal your willingness to negotiate or listen to their complaints. Stand or sit in a relaxed fashion without slouching, which indicates submission. Smile sincerely and nod gently to assure the person you are listening attentively.

- Walking with their arms swinging loosely by their sides is a sign that they are comfortable, at ease, secure, and happy with the way life is going.
    - Enjoy the companionship and ease of the relationship.
    - Respond with similar body language as well as verbal affirmation that you are comfortable and happy with the relationship, too.
- Using their arms and hands to push you away signals that they don't want you in their personal space.
    - This is rarely something you will experience outside of a parent/child relationship. Therefore, it is rarely acceptable to allow your child to push you away. But if they do, you need to discern why. This usually involves verbal communication.
    - Before the problem can be addressed and solved, however, you will need to deescalate the situation by calming your child down. This might involve wrapping them in a hug or taking their hands in yours and reminding them that pushing is not acceptable.
    - Once the child is calm enough to listen rationally you need to use both your body and your words to calm them, reassure them, and lead them in the right direction—the direction of making good choices and decisions. Your body language needs to tell them they are safe and that you care about how they feel, and you

will do what you can to help them. You can do this by keeping your body 'soft,' as in relaxed. Breathe slowly and deeply. Seeing your chest rise and fall slowly and feeling the slower rhythm of your breathing will cause them to do the same. Smile softly. Stroke their back, the top of their head or their upper arm gently and slowly. Snuggle with your young child to 'shield' them from whatever is causing them to act out.

- o There are times you need to honor their request to step out of their personal space. They need to know that pushing you away isn't the way to make that happen, but once you establish that fact, you need to respect their need for space—physically and emotionally.

- If you move toward someone and they position their arms firmly at their sides, put them behind their back or pick something up, they are saying they do not want to be hugged or touched. They would prefer that you keep your distance.

  - o This one is simple. Honor their request.

- If you move toward someone and they lean forward a bit, open their arms (even partially), or extend one or both arms, they are saying they will reciprocate a hug, handshake, fist bump or other similar greeting.

  - o This one is pretty simple, too. Respond appropriately. Respond with genuine warmth and sincerity.

- Nail biting, cracking/popping their knuckles, or twisting hair are all signs of nervousness. They are subconscious acts, though, so people don't usually realize they are telling on themselves.
  - Put people at ease with your body language. Smile, make eye contact, listen attentively, don't cross your arms, furrow your brows or send any other signal that can be interpreted as intimidating.
  - Do a visual assessment of the situation and surroundings. If you can determine the source of their nervousness and you have the ability to alleviate it, do so. If you are able to determine the source of their nervousness but cannot do anything to 'make it all better,' let them know you care and that you are there to help however you can.
- Shrugging their shoulders indicates an attitude of indifference and disinterest.
  - This is another case of picking your battles. If the situation isn't of great importance or causing someone to disrespect you or others, let it go.
  - If, on the other hand, the person's actions are expressly rude and disrespectful, acknowledge that you respect their different point of view, but that they need to return the 'favor.'
  - Depending on the subject matter and the type of relationship you share with this person,

engage them in a discussion to respectfully share your differences of opinion. Who knows? One or both of you may actually learn something.

Body and posture

Tuna Harbor Park, which is located near the USS Midway and is part of Navy Pier in San Diego, is home to a twenty-five-foot-tall statue replicating the forever-famous photograph that has been dubbed "Unconditional Surrender." You know which photograph I'm talking about, don't you? It's the one of the WWII sailor kissing the nurse in Times Square on VJ (Victory over Japan) Day. 'Unconditional' is the key word. There is nothing about the nurse's posture to indicate she is anything less than 'all in' for the iconic embrace and kiss captured on film for all the world to see and admire then, now, and probably forever.

In stark contrast is a photo I saw recently of a group of children—my friend's grandchildren. The only boy in the group of six, who was two or three, was clearly 'done.' While all the girls were posed with smiles on their faces, Silas was crying and walking away from the group. It's a great picture and one they all laugh about now and 'threaten' to recreate the next time they're all together.

Both pictures tell a lot about the people in them. Just by looking at the pictures we can discern moods, attitudes, emotions, and even a level of intellect. So, pay attention to the people around you. Don't let yourself be disillusioned or misled because you weren't able to read their body language.

- Turning away from you when you speak to someone is a sign of their defiance, distrust, or disinterest. The specifics of the situation will tell you which it is.
    - If defiance is the problem, you need to address the issue by presenting yourself as fair but firm. You can do this by standing or sitting up straight, making and maintaining eye contact, leaning forward with your arms and legs 'open' versus crossed, and making sure your face is relaxed instead of wearing a scowl.
    - If distrust is the problem, your body language needs to reassure them that you are trustworthy and truthful. Maintain eye contact, don't shuffle your feet, or put your hands to your face while you are talking. If appropriate, a reassuring hand on the shoulder or taking their hand in yours can also build trust.
    - If disinterest is the problem, the best thing you can do is cut the conversation short by giving them only the facts they need to know (if any) and stop talking. You should also present yourself as confident and enthusiastic or purposeful (depending on what you have to say). Stand or sit up straight, but not stiff. Relax your facial muscles. If you use your hands, keep your movements smooth and fluid. Don't cross your arms or point your finger at them.
    - Dragging things out and/or trying to win them over often ends up making things worse. Sometimes it's a matter of that person having

a bad day or not feeling well. If you discern that this is the case, drop the matter (unless it is essential that they know). A handshake or pat on the back, along with a smile and a nod tells the person you are not offended by them.

- Reclining back on their elbows with their legs stretched out in front of them tells you that the person you are with is relaxed, comfortable, and feels safe, secure, and confident.
    - o This is the sign of a close, comfortable, intimate relationship. The intimacy may or may not be of the romantic/sexual kind. It may be a BFF brand of intimacy or the intimacy between a parent/child, siblings or between you and other extended family members. Whichever it is, this posture tells you that you can trust the one you are with and that they can trust you, so take advantage of these times (in a good way) to have heart-to-heart conversations, confide in one another, seek advice, plan and prepare for the future or any combination of all of them.
    - o When someone has opened themselves to you like this, you need to be careful not to betray them by saying something different with your body. Let yourself relax too, and use your facial expressions, gentle touches, eye contact, and welcoming gestures (open palms, uncrossed arms and legs) to let them know you are as committed to the relationship as they are.

- Standing or sitting with their shoulders back and their chest out says that person is confident, sure of their position, and in control of their thoughts and feelings.
  - If you observe this body language in your child, you are obviously doing something right in the parenting department, so go ahead and give yourself a pat on the back. As parents we all want to raise our children to be confident and unafraid to stand on their own two feet when it comes to deciding who and what they are.
  - As far as responses go when speaking and interacting with someone whose body is sending these signals, respect and acknowledgment that their thoughts and opinions matter is in order. You can do this by maintaining eye contact with them while they are speaking, lean in slightly to signify you are listening attentively, and give a slight nod now and then to let them know you understand what they are saying.
  - Respect and acknowledgement doesn't always equal agreement with what someone is saying, though, does it? If this is the case, make sure you do the things listed above, but when they are done speaking, let them know you would like (and expect) equal opportunity and respect to share your views. You, too, should stand or sit confidently with squared shoulders and your chest out slightly. Stay calm; don't shuffle

or tap your feet. If sitting, place your hands (unfolded) in your lap or on your thighs with the palms down. These things signal that you, too, are confident in your beliefs, but are not in the frame of mind to challenge anyone—that this is nothing more than a time of sharing and letting each other know where you stand on an issue.

- When someone is sitting with their legs crossed, it indicates a need for privacy and an unwillingness to engage in conversation beyond what is obligatory. The reason may be as simple as not feeling well or not being in the mood. But it could also be a matter of not trusting you to take them seriously or to keep their confidence.

    o If they are not feeling well or not in the mood to have the conversation at that particular time, you need to respect this and wait. Letting the matter rest and possibly even offering to help them feel better can work to build their trust and confidence in you for future conversations and interactions.

    o If a lack of trust is the issue, you need to establish the reason or reasons for this. Then, once you have done so, you need to take whatever actions you can to remedy the situation. This could take time, so be patient.

- When the person you are talking to leans into you from a standing or sitting position, with their arms planted firmly at their sides or crossed in front of them, they

are declaring their independence and letting you know they feel confident and in control of the situation. There could possibly be an element of rebellion involved—especially if the interaction is with your preteen or teenager or with someone (a student, employer, employee, or someone else wanting to challenge your authority). If this is the case, your body language needs to reflect back to them that you are not going to allow them to intimidate you BUT that you are willing to listen and take their grievances into consideration. You can do this by:
  - Standing or sitting up straight; leaning forward just a bit.
  - Maintaining eye contact and keeping your eyes wide open and slightly raising your brow to indicate interest and intent listening.
  - A 'soft' mouth (neither smiling nor frowning).
  - Do not cross your arms or your legs.

- Fidgeting while sitting or standing is a sign that the person you are with is uncomfortable. Their discomfort usually stems from one of the following: dishonesty, shyness, anxiety over being the center of attention, being put on the spot or from being out of their comfort zone. A smile, relaxed posture, uncrossed arms, and possibly even placing a reassuring hand on their shoulder or holding their hand in yours usually works to put the person at ease. This is especially true when you back up your body language with words of encouragement and understanding.

- Sitting (or possibly even standing) in a slumped position is fairly common among teenagers and young adults. It usually means they are at ease and comfortable with their surroundings. Their sense of comfort usually comes from a feeling of familiarity and security, which is a good thing. Sometimes, however, it is a sign of laziness and lack of interest and motivation. Their facial expressions and verbal interaction will let you know which scenario you are dealing with.

- o If they stare at you blankly, roll their eyes or won't make eye contact, you can safely assume they are uninterested in what is going on or what you have to say.

- o If they smile, cock their head to one side or relax their body even more, you will know they are glad to be a part of whatever is going on.

- One of the least desirable statements a person can make with their body is to be curled up in the fetal position. Almost without exception it is a signal of distress on some level. Pain/illness. Fear. Grief. Anxiety. Depression. Despondency. A mechanism of self-defense. Escape. Admission of defeat. Someone in the fetal position should never be put on hold or ignored. Even if it is something as simple as an acute case of nausea. Hey, we've all been there. When you feel that bad you are desperate for help. Right? So don't ever make light of someone in this position. They need and deserve your attention.

  - o When someone is in the fetal position the first thing you need to do is determine why. Once you do that, you can decide how to proceed.

- You need to remember that using your body language to speak back to them will be minimal, but nevertheless important. A smile, a hug or holding them close, a firm, but gentle hand to guide and steady their steps, a soothing touch to the back, stroking their hair, or simply sitting close enough to let them lean on you can literally be lifesaving.

- Body language, however, is rarely enough to deal with these situations. Verbal confirmation of the problem, as well as offering comfort, advice, information, and/or counseling will undoubtedly be in order, as well.

Legs and feet

I dare you…I double-dog dare you to watch the "Trolls" movie without tapping your toes to the music or even getting up to dance around the room. Seriously, I don't think anyone—not even the grouchy lunchroom lady could resist that one.

Here is something else I recently witnessed: A mom was walking around the room gently bouncing her baby to quiet him. After a few minutes, *her* mom (the baby's grandma) took the baby and did the same to give the momma a break. But guess what? Momma stopped walking around the room, but she kept gently bouncing in place. After a good two or three minutes she started laughing and said, "I have no idea why I'm still bouncing. I'm not the one who was fussing."

In this case the young momma's body language didn't stop talking. Her legs kept right on bouncing out the message, "I'm here for you. You're safe and sound—there's no need to cry."

Our bodies have a way of telling on us. They reveal what we subconsciously and consciously think and feel. That is why it is important to listen with your ears and your eyes. Otherwise, you might miss something important—something that can alter the outcome of a conversation greatly. One way or the other.

- Stepping in place from one foot to another indicates boredom, being ill at ease, and impatience. This might stem from shyness, a lack of honesty or disinterest in what is going on.

- Tapping their foot slowly indicates they are thinking about what is being said or planning their next move.

- Tapping their foot quickly is a sign of impatience.

- Repeatedly raising up on their tiptoes and then falling back on flat feet is a sign that your teenager is trying to do better. Reach higher (figuratively speaking).

- Shuffling their feet is a sign a teenager is ill at ease. They may be shy, afraid of being 'found out,' or bored. They are subconsciously trying to 'escape.'

- Standing rigidly indicates either anger or fear. The specifics of the situation along with other body language will tell you which it is.

- Rocking back and forth on their heels is a sign of boredom. They can't wait to get away.

- Standing or sitting with their knees turned in and pressed together says they are not going to let you invade their privacy. They are trying to protect their personal space.

Take a minute to reread a statement made earlier in this chapter: It is important to listen with your ears and your eyes. Otherwise, you might miss something important—something that can alter the outcome of a conversation greatly. One way or the other. Now I want to expound on that by saying that not only does body language have the potential to alter the outcome of a conversation but can alter the course of a relationship, as well. One way or the other.

Conduct a little research. Make a mental note of the body language people use this week while talking to you. After the conversation (because it would be awkward to do it while you are talking to them) record the following information:

- Their overall posture
- Movements and position of their hands and arms
- Movements and position of their legs and feet
- Facial expressions

Now, compare their body language to the actual conversation. Do the two match up? For example, if the conversation was pleasant and productive, did the person smile? Were they relaxed and unafraid to make eye contact with you? Or if you were disciplining your child, did they shuffle their feet, or look in any direction but toward you?

Visit the following website: 13 Passages from Children's Literature that are More Dreadful and Shocking Than They

May First Appear | HuffPost Read each of the quotes from the classic books given in the article. While reading:

a) Imagine the scene (or recall it in your mind's eye if you've watched the movie based on the book). What body language do you think is being spoken?
b) Be conscious of your own body language while reading each passage. How does your body react to the words you read?

CHAPTER EIGHT
BODY LANGUAGE IN THE WORKPLACE

"Don't waste time learning the "tricks of the trade." Instead, learn the trade."
~ Attributed to James Charlton

We are going to spend the next few pages looking at some examples of body language in the workplace. To do that we are going to recall scenes from movies and televisions shows, books, and some real-life examples of things that take place on the job. We'll cover a variety of perspectives:

- The employer
- The employee
- Onlookers
- Students
- Customers and clients
- Those with experience
- Those who are wet behind the ears
- Someone whose heart is in the right place
- Someone whose only interest is looking out for themselves
- The workplace a few decades ago
- The workplace today

The scenarios and people involved will come from a variety of backgrounds. The desired outcomes will be different depending on both the situation and the people involved. But one thing will be consistently the same across time, generations, sexes, ethnicity, geography, and socioeconomics: body language.

NOTE: The following examples are not in any order of importance or relevance and no favoritism is being shown to any one publisher, producer or sales source. They are merely examples used to demonstrate the reality of body language and the role it plays in our careers and in the workplace.

To Kill a Mockingbird

We're going to look at two characters in this book/movie. We're going to look at Atticus Finch and Calpurnia "Cal."

First let's look at Atticus Finch. Atticus is a single (widowed) father to his son Jem and his daughter Scout in the deep south (Alabama) during the dark days of the Great Depression (1932). He is firm but fair, patient, loving, and kind, but never overly permissive or lax in what he expects of his children.

Atticus is also a highly respected lawyer and citizen of their community. It is in the courtroom and outside the jail house late one night that we see just how powerful body language can be.

The courthouse: Atticus has willingly taken on the task of defending a black man falsely accused of committing a crime against a young white woman. Outside the courtroom he experiences raised eyebrows, sneers, jeers, and threats against his life. But Atticus doesn't let that stop him from commanding respect and authority in the courtroom (or out of it, for that matter). He stands tall and erect. He holds his head up high. He refuses to break eye contact with the accuser, her father, and members of the jury. BUT Atticus doesn't command this respect by way of intimidation. He doesn't lean into the accuser or tower over her (even though he could). He doesn't cross his arms to signify his refusal to hear or consider what she has to say. But make no mistake about it—he lets her know via his words, the look on his face, and the confidence in his movements that he knows the truth.

Outside the jail: At one point a mob comes to take matters into their own hands, vigilante-style. Atticus had gotten wind of the plan, so he is waiting for them; calmly sitting outside Tom's (his client's) jail cell. When the angry mob of men arrive Atticus doesn't flinch. He holds his ground by standing tall and resolute and looking them straight in the eye. When he doesn't flinch, fidget, or cower—not in the least, the mob leaves.

Atticus Finch's body language in the workplace leaves no room for doubt that he is a man of honor and integrity, and that nothing will stop him from doing his job to the best of his ability and to the fullest extent the law will allow.

Calpurnia "Cal" is the housekeeper/nanny to Jem and Scout Finch. Cal performs her duties with confidence and obvious love and concern for the family. She isn't afraid to give Scout 'the look' when her table manners are less than appropriate, and she nods understandingly when a conversation with Atticus leads to questions the children didn't need to ask and information Atticus didn't want them made privy to.

Cal's body language in the workplace, which is the Finch home, leaves no question in the hearts and minds of Atticus,

Jem, and Scout that she doesn't see her position as just a job. She genuinely cares for and loves the children and is a loyal and dedicated 'surrogate' member of the family.

Takeaway: Confidence in the workplace comes from knowing your job and knowing it well. In turn, that confidence gives you the backbone (literally and figuratively speaking) to stand or sit straight and tall, perform your duties adeptly, receive the respect and trust of others, and enjoy a sense of fulfillment that you are living and working purposefully.

9 to 5

This blockbuster movie was a groundbreaking comedy. The movie was released in 1980—a time when the number of women in the workplace was changing rapidly. The movie's three main characters, Judy, Violet, and Doralee, come from three drastically different backgrounds, but their goal is the same—to be respected and appreciated in the workplace. And among other things, they use body language to make sure that happens.

At the onset, **Judy's** body language makes it difficult for anyone to take her seriously. As a recent divorcee, the job is her first experience in the workplace—a proverbial fish out of water. She has trouble making eye contact, she is jittery and clumsy, and she flounders around trying to look surer of herself than she actually is. She fails miserably.

Next is **Violet.** Violet has been on the job for a while. She is capable, knowledgeable, and competent. But because she lacks the confidence to put herself out there, she is treated like a doormat by the boss (a man) and the woman in the office bent on being as close to the top of the ladder as possible.

Violet swallows the bait of self-doubt hook, line, and sinker. Her body language screams, "Walk all over me because I don't have the courage or strength to stop you." She cowers, plays her pencil like a drum, doesn't make eye contact, scurries around like a scared mouse, and makes some critical (albeit comical) errors.

Last but not least is **Doralee.** Doralee is the bold and confident one of the trio. She has to be, because as the boss's private secretary she has to fend off his constant sexual advances. Doralee uses her body language (not her body parts) to defend herself and to send the message that her value to the company lies in her job skills and her ability to do her job. She looks people in the eye, she moves with deliberate confidence, and she is always aware of her surroundings. And she is not the least bit afraid to use her hands and feet to physically defend her honor.

Takeaway: Confidence is key when it comes to being taken seriously in the workplace. You have to walk, stand, sit, and speak with confidence. Don't confuse confidence with arrogance or being a bully, but don't be afraid to stand up for yourself. Very few people (at best) will bother looking past the obvious to see what you aren't saying (with your body or your words). So, it is up to you to make sure your body sends the message you want it to, because your body language is a PSA of sorts, announcing what you have to offer.

The body language vocabulary you need to send that message includes walking and sitting with squared shoulders and a lifted chin. You need to offer genuine smiles to coworkers, listen attentively to both superiors and coworkers, and be a team player. When someone contradicts, opposes, or treats you unfairly don't cower, but don't come out fighting, either. Let your body show you are willing to engage in conversation and conflict resolution by keeping your body fluid and open (no crossed arms or crossed legs; speak with palms up and open instead of clenching your fists and pointing your finger). And just in case someone doesn't know how or bothers to read your body language (which is often the case), don't be afraid to back it up with words.

John—real life law enforcement officer

Spending thirty years as a state law enforcement road officer left John with enough stories to tell concerning his encounters with people and their body language to be a book all on their own. But when asked to share a few that left a deeper impression than others, here is what he had to say:

"One night I got a call to respond and assist with a possible break-in at a local veterinary clinic. When I arrived, I found that someone had driven their car through the clinic's plate glass window. My initial assumption was that it was a case of someone desperate for drugs. But in a matter of seconds, I learned that wasn't the case at all. What happened was that a sixteen-year-old boy who'd gotten his license the day before accidentally hit the gas instead of the break to avoid running a stop sign he almost didn't see because he was busy messing with his phone. I will never forget the look on his face when I shined my flashlight into the shattered window. He was terrified and had his hands raised in the air. And the first words out of his mouth were, "Please don't tell my dad."

It took everything I had not to smile…laugh, even. But I didn't. Instead, I instructed him to come forward; keeping his hands where I could see them. Once he was out of the building and I ascertained that his story was true, I actually felt sorry for him. He curled up like a rag doll; scared to death to face what was going to happen next. The officer in me remained objective and matter of fact, but the dad in me calmly and gently reassured the boy that he was fortunate in that no one or no one's pet had been hurt or killed.

Doc (the owner of the clinic) and the boy's dad were both there by that time and when Doc saw the boy and learned what happened, he offered to work out a deal with the kid to work off the damage. The boy and his dad humbly and gratefully accepted the offer. Doc's offer also changed the dad's demeanor. His body language told us that he'd recovered from the initial surge of shock and anger and was now ready to deal with the incident as a father should—with grace and to use it as a lesson in responsibility instead of using it as a weapon against the boy."

Unfortunately, more often than not, the element of humor couldn't be found in most of the experiences John had. For example…

"It was always frustrating and heartbreaking to hear a woman tell you that everything was okay when the fear in her eyes, her trembling body, and the way she tucked her head into her shoulders—not to mention the bruises—told you that everything was NOT okay. But I couldn't help her if she said she didn't need help.

And even though I can't begin to count the number of death calls I went on—knocking on someone's door to tell them their loved one has died—I will never forget having to tell my close friend who just happened to be the mechanic for our troop, that his son, a fellow officer, had been killed in a head-on crash. Holding him in my arms while he sobbed and moaned is something I will never forget. Not ever. The happy-go-lucky guy who always walked with a spring in his step and a twinkle in his eye was gone. And even though it's been nearly twenty years since that horrible day, Newt's body language—especially his eyes—tells you that even though life goes on after tragedy strikes, pain is now part of the journey, too."

Takeaway: There are certain types of jobs—law enforcement, lawyers, social workers, and nurses, for example—that require you to distance yourself emotionally. Your effectiveness and professional excellence will suffer if you get emotionally involved. But that doesn't mean you cannot feel or that you cannot and should not let people see you as compassionate, fair, and willing to listen.

When you are in a position of authority, your body language should never say anything to lead someone to think otherwise. And it won't as long as you stand erect with squared shoulders, and keep your body turned toward the person or people you are in charge of. It is also essential to make sure your facial expressions mirror what you say (the knowledge and expertise you possess to do your job well). But don't be afraid or too indifferent to let the people you serve know that you are human, too. An encouraging smile, nods of approval, a handshake, a gentle touch, and taking the time to listen attentively sometimes makes your job easier. By taking the lead when it comes to responding in a positive manner often causes the other person/people to reciprocate in the same way.

The Freedom Writers

First a book and then a movie, the *Freedom Writers* is a heartwarming example of why reading someone's body language is so important, and why body language often reveals a truer message than the words that come out of our mouths.

In a nutshell, *Freedom Writers* is the true story of a fresh-out-of-college schoolteacher, Erin Gruwell. Ms. Gruwell's first teaching assignment is a high school freshmen English class in Long Beach, CA, at Woodrow Wilson High. Her students come from a mixed bag of ethnic and socioeconomic backgrounds. Few (almost none) expectations had been placed on them regarding their academic achievements and future. Until Erin arrives on the scene, that is.

Erin Gruwell recognizes the body language in these kids that said things like:

- "No one else cares, so why should I?"
- "This is a waste of time. I'm going to end up just like my mom/dad, anyway."
- "Street-smarts are the only education I need to survive."
- "It doesn't matter what I want or what hopes and dreams I have. They can't come true."

So, she challenges them. She pushes hard and when they push back, she pushes back even harder. And in the process both the students and school administrators learn to read Erin's body language. Language that says:

- "I'm not afraid of you."
- "I'm not going to give up on you."
- "Stop wallowing in self-pity and stand up for yourself."
- "I'm in charge so pay attention."
- "As long as you are in my classroom, we're going to do things my way."
- "I believe in you. You have talent and potential and I'm not going to let you throw it away."

Once Erin and her students started paying attention to and responding to each other's body language things changed. Lives changed—forever and for the good.

Takeaway: Teachers, professors, coaches, business and store managers, and even a lot of parents these days are intimidated by their students, employees, and children. Your body language shows it, giving people permission to disrespect you.

You are the only one who can put a stop to this, so do it! Look people in the eye. Don't 'hide' behind a desk, podium or chair. Walk without shuffling. Don't fall back on nervous habits like biting your nails, tapping a pencil or your fingers or biting your lip. Go about the business of completing tasks with smooth but precise motions, instead of procrastinating or doing things half-way. Remember: You are a leader, so stand, sit, think, act, and speak like one.

Gary—real life preacher

When Gary started preaching back in the early 1960s, he and his young family were welcomed into their first congregation with open arms—literally. Hugs were as much a part of saying hello and goodbye on Sunday and Wednesday as handshakes were. That's just the way it was in their small, close-knit church family. Gary, who was a father himself, thought nothing of tossing the little ones up in the air then bringing them in for a hug; or if he was first on the scene, so to speak, to kiss a boo-boo 'all better.' Each summer during the two weeks he always spent teaching kids and teens at church camp, he didn't think twice about blocking or slamming the volleyball, dousing both boys and girls during water-wars or hugging the young person just baptized into Christ. But by the time Gary retired in the early 2000s, things had changed. A lot. And in his words, "It breaks my heart."

As Gary sat visiting with the young man who was going to take over Gary's position as preacher and minister of the same church he'd started at over forty years earlier, he was dismayed and astonished by one conversation he had with the young man. The conversation focused on the importance of a preacher/minister not sending the wrong signals with his body language.

When Gary asked what constituted a wrong signal, the younger man explained they were taught not to hug anyone between the age of three and younger than their own mother. The exception was when expressing their condolences or welcoming them to the Church, but even then, it was to be done only briefly and in public. He then went on to give Gary a few other particulars.

Afterward, Gary sighed and said, "It's sad that even the people of God's Church are afraid to speak to one another using more than words. I can't begin to count the times that a hug, a hand squeeze, an arm around their shoulders or freely offering my shoulder to cry on has gotten someone through a dark day or night. And I am not afraid or ashamed to say I think we're headed in a wrong direction. If people don't feel they can literally lean on you, they won't. And when that stops happening the Church is going to suffer greatly."

Takeaway: While there are most certainly circumstances and incidents in which people from a wide variety of professions in positions of authority and leadership have abused their position and have perverted the reputation attached to their position, Gary was right. It's sad—tragic, even—that we are being cautioned against and instructed on how not to care. How not to express genuine concern, compassion, appreciation, and gratitude. Words are important. They always have been and always will be. But actions, aka body language,

DO speak louder than words. So, if you are a member of the clergy, a coach, scout leader, funeral director, counselor, hospice or home healthcare worker, coach, social worker or some other profession in which you are involved with people on a personal level, don't be afraid or unwilling to let your body language sing in harmony with your words.

- Keep your hugs from appearing too intimate by hugging only from the arms up. In other words, maintain a few inches of distance between you and the other person below the shoulders and chest area.
- Don't kiss a child that isn't yours over the age of two and only then, on the top of the head.
- A gentle and brief hand squeeze, a hand on the arm or back or an arm around the shoulders should last only a few seconds.
- Keep your body turned toward the person you are with, but maintain a few inches of space between you.
- If the person 'falls into you' seeking comfort and support in a time of grief or fear, do not reject them, but don't prolong the encounter. Gently place your hands on their shoulders and gently put some distance between you. Explain to them that this will better enable you to listen and speak to them.
- If someone makes an inappropriate move toward you, or one you know can be chalked up to 'the heat of the moment,' don't make the situation worse by lashing out. Remain calm but let your words and your actions send a clear message that you are not interested in taking things any farther. Then excuse yourself, keep your distance from that person, avoid any contact other than in public/group situations, and depending

on the situation, it might be wise to confide in someone you can trust explicitly—someone who can vouch for you and your integrity. Don't wait to go to someone, though. If you feel you need to talk to someone, do it right away. Not only will the facts be clearer in your mind, but it will serve to collaborate your whereabouts as a sort of timeline of events.

- Don't ever be afraid to smile, give a reassuring nod or a high-five/thumb's up. Encouragement and recognition are oxygen to our soul, and we can never get too much.

The Andy Griffith Show

You can't talk about body language in the workplace without talking about the clumsy, over-zealous, and well-meaning Deputy Sheriff Barney Fife. You can't help but love him. Laugh at him. Get aggravated with him. Be glad you don't have to work with him.

No one took him seriously. Why would they? On the outside he was confident and sure of himself. But it was all talk. He was timid, nervous, jumped to conclusions without getting the facts, and was as unskilled and unfit for the position as a person could get. And it showed. Boy did it ever! He was completely unaware of his surroundings. He slouched, twitched, fidgeted, and fumbled around. He dropped and lost things on several occasions, and when someone challenged him he physically and mentally shrank down a size or two.

But all that aside we can actually learn a lot from good ole Barney. No, seriously, we can.

Takeaway: The things we can take away from Deputy Barney Fife are:

- Know your job, i.e., be thoroughly trained to do your job and do it well.
- Use your job skills with confidence. Your movements and actions need to be deliberate and precise. Whether you are taking someone's blood pressure, presenting a proposal at city council, showing a house to potential buyers or guiding a bride-to-be through deciding what to serve at the reception, your body language needs to let other people know that you believe in yourself and your level of capability to serve them.
- Don't let people's criticisms intimidate you. Even if they are justified statements, don't run and hide like a turtle retreating into its shell. Own your mistake and/or admit you need help or instruction, but present yourself in such a way that says you are capable of handling the added knowledge and responsibility.
- Don't let your nervousness show—especially to those under your leadership or those you have authority over. No one will take you seriously if you appear unsure and incapable.
- Don't accept a position or responsibilities you aren't ready for. Your body language will give you away; giving people yet another reason to not take you seriously and giving yourself another reason to doubt your value and worth.

The Book of Lost Names

This book takes place in Europe during WWII. It is based on the true story of heroism in which a young Jewish woman conspires with a priest and a man who ends up being the love of her life, to forge the identities of hundreds of Jewish children in order to save their lives.

In order to do so, she must meticulously forge thousands of pages of documents such as birth certificates, ration books, and so forth to the degree that they convince the Nazis that these children are not Jewish. In order to do that though, the children's names have to be changed. They have to be given a new name—a less Jewish sounding name—which means the name they were given at birth by the parents who love them enough to give them this chance at life, must be erased from existence.

The thought of this is more than Eva can stand, so together with her forging partner and true love, they come up with a secret code that records each child's real name; matching it with their forged identification.

It really is an amazing story, but here's the point to be made for the role body language played in the success of this undertaking.

- Eva had to have a steady hand…a very steady hand. Her movements had to be precise and consistent. Otherwise, countless lives would have been lost.
- Eva always had to carry herself (walk, stand, shop, greet people, etc.) outwardly confident. No shuffling, twitches, darting glances, nervous nail biting or trembling hands were allowed. People's lives (including hers) depended upon her ability to present herself as benign and 'harmless' to the Nazi regime.
- Eva had to be aware of her surroundings without seeming to be. She always had to be looking ahead and

scanning the area around her to gauge if she was being watched or in danger.

Confident. Precise. Consistent. Dependable. Aware. Conscious. Capable. Sure. All of these qualities can be observed and verified by your body language. You can also be sure that employers pick up on these things—sometimes without even thinking about it. I guess you could say they speak without being spoken to first.

Takeaway: Your body language's ability to convince your boss, coworkers, clients/customers, potential employers, and even family and friends of your ability, sincerity, and commitment to something is invaluable. It is something you should never take for granted. For although one would hope and pray it is never a matter of life or death, it can (and often does) determine whether or not you get a job, a promotion, make the sale, seal the deal or enjoy a healthy, fulfilling relationship, versus the opposite on all counts.

I hope you enjoyed looking at the different scenarios of how body language works for or against you in the workplace. More importantly I hope you are ready, willing, and able to put it to use for you so that you can aspire to your full potential in your chosen field.

CHAPTER NINE
BODY LANGUAGE AS A MEANS OF SELF-DEFENSE

"Cultivate a habit of caution." ~ Safety saying, circa early 1900s

Possessing a keen and accurate awareness of your surroundings is an important 'piece of equipment' to have in your life's survival kit (figuratively speaking). Being aware, i.e., seeing and sensing possible danger is often THE thing that keeps an accident or crime from making you a victim. But what *is* awareness and how do we have or get it? In one word: OBSERVATION. In two words: OBSERVATION and RESPONSE.

Most of the time, possible dilemmas and dangers can be averted and avoided by simply noticing (observing) that something isn't right, and then either making a correction or removing yourself from the situation.

Body language plays a huge role in how successful you are in defending yourself against such things. Not only do you need to be using YOUR body language to seek out and discern what is and isn't safe, but you also need to be reading other peoples' body language in order to determine whether or not they pose a risk to you/your safety.

By now you know that most of the time body language is a subconscious way of speaking. We use our posture, facial expressions, movements of our hands, arms, feet and legs, and even our breathing patterns to convey our true thoughts and feelings. The way we carry ourselves speaks volumes. That is why, when it comes to self-defense, we need to make sure our body is sending the message that says, "Don't mess with me." AND that we are reading the body language of the people around us looking for those who might be saying, "You're my next target," "You look like easy prey," or "I want what you have and I'm not afraid to take it from you."

We've already spent a considerable amount of time talking about how and what we need to do to send the messages we want to send. So, for the sake of not sounding like a broken record, we're going to spend the majority of our time in this chapter discussing what we need to look for in others in an effort to defend ourselves against them.

Before we get into it though, I want to remind you not to fall for the false assumption that things like this (accidents and crimes) only happen to other people. Think about it—to someone else YOU are other people. You could be:

- One of the 1 in 5 women who will be raped at some point in their life.
- One of the 50% of women who will be the victim of a sexual assault other than rape in their lifetime.

OR...

- One of the 1 in 71 men who will be raped at some point in their life.
- One of the 1 in 5 men who will be the victim of a sexual assault other than rape in their lifetime.

So don't be lured into a false sense of security because it's not worth the risk. It's just not.

Let's start with what YOUR body needs to say.

Face:

The body language of the face is the most complex. Not complex in that it is the most difficult to read, but complex in that it can say so much. The face's body language is also unique in that a lot of it can be consciously controlled and some of it cannot. You've probably heard the phrase 'poker face' to describe what we're talking about. For example, the mom of a precarious toddler usually has the necessary amount of self-control to keep the smile off her face when he says something comical out of context or at a most inopportune time. A teenager trying to hide their guilt, however, will not be able to keep their eyes fixed on you for fear you'll see right through them.

The information you need to impart using your facial body language includes:

Pupil dilation: The fight or flight message your pupils relay is something few people can control. The brain signals the body to deposit adrenaline into the bloodstream to increase your heart rate. The increased heart rate dilates (enlarges) the pupils. Enlarged pupils decrease the range of your peripheral vision, which in turn makes it necessary for you to look directly at someone in order to actually see them.

If fear or intimidation is the reasoning behind the issue, the only recourse we have is to be unafraid and unintimidated. But if you are in danger of being bullied, abused or attacked, that is not going to happen. You can (and should), however, try to mask the extent of your anxiety or fear by breathing more slowly. Here's what happens. By taking **slow *deep* breaths** you increase the amount of oxygen going into the bloodstream, which in turn slows down the heartrate, which then reduces the amount of adrenaline in the bloodstream and shrinks the pupils of your eyes.

When an assailant sees less fear in your eyes, they tend to become less forceful, but that usually only lasts for a brief period of time. It's as if they are trying to understand why you aren't afraid of them. But even that brief period of time can be enough for you to make a move that will hopefully change the outcome of the situation significantly…and in your favor.

FYI: The slower breathing, etc., doesn't have to just mask your true feelings. It can actually give you a sense of empowerment. By taking control of your breathing, you are essentially taking better control over your whole self—body and mind. And in those split seconds, you can actually develop the courage and strength you need to survive an awful ordeal.

Sweating: This is something completely out of our control. Sweating is an involuntary action that happens when our body temperature rises for any number of reasons. Sweat is the body's coolant system if you will. So, generally speaking, sweat is the body language 'word' for, "I'm hot."

We all know there are several reasons why and ways to increase our body's temperature. But since we're talking about self-defense the one we are going to focus on is anxiety/fear/stress. You already know that experiencing any or all of these emotions causes the heartrate to increase. So along with adrenaline being pumped into the bloodstream when our heartrate increases, the increase also causes the sweat glands located throughout the body to start working. Unfortunately, the slowed breathing technique doesn't work as quickly or as well to decrease or stop us from sweating out of fear. That means the only way to reduce the chances of sweat sending a message to a possible assailant is to be proactive in making sure other parts of your body speak the message that says, "I'm ready to defend myself" loud and clear.

Eyes: The eyes have two completely different jobs, so to speak, when it comes to self-defense. The first job is to read your surroundings in an effort to prevent yourself from being bullied, abused or attacked. Your eyes need to read what other people are saying with their bodies so you can decide whether to go into a building, walk down a street in a particular direction, not stop for coffee or take whatever steps are necessary to calmly end a relationship.

That's a lot of responsibility to place on two small body parts but trust me—they can do it if you use them properly.

- Observe how someone you are romantically interested in treats their mother and father. This is a strong indicator of how they will treat you.
- What is the tone of someone's social media posts? What they post and share says a LOT about who they really are. Knowing these things is a means of self-defense against bullying and abusive friendships/relationships.
- Be watchful of strangers who suddenly and/or deliberately move to block your path, cross over to your side of the street or walk toward you with obvious intentions of engaging you in some manner.

- Use your eyes to scan your surroundings before proceeding into a parking garage, parking lot or other area with few or no other people around.
- Use your eyes to always make sure there is no one in your car before you get in.
- Use your eyes to assess the entryway of your house/apartment before going inside.
- Use your eyes to observe how someone reacts to being corrected, rejection or annoyances such as a slow or clumsy waitress, long checkout lines, etc. These things will tell you a lot about how a person will respond to you when you make mistakes, hurt their feelings or fail to meet their expectations.
- Use your eyes to scout out safe surroundings when choosing a parking spot, a walking or jogging route or when going into a public restroom. Can you park near a security booth, an entry or exit or under a light? Is the path you want to walk/jog well-lit and well-traveled during the times you like to go? And are there few, if any, hiding places assailants can lie in wait from? Do you notice anyone just hanging around the bathroom area who obviously isn't waiting for someone to rejoin them?

Using your eyes to observe these things (and more) to read someone else's body language is a means of self-defense that too many people don't use to the extent they should. If that weren't the case, the number of incidents would decline drastically.

Now let's go in the other direction where the eyes are concerned. Let's look at how we can use our eyes to defend ourselves against an assailant in the heat of the moment.

- Look your assailant in the eye. No matter how scared you are and no matter how repulsive it may be, do everything in your power to maintain eye contact with them. Keeping **eye contact with someone who is trying to inflict harm on you intimidates them.** It also **makes them fearful of being more easily identified for prosecution.** The mindset of an assailant is that they are bigger and badder than you, so they can take what they want simply because you can't stop them. But **when you look them in the eye you are diluting their sense of bigness and badness.** Or as I've often heard it said, you would be "cutting them down to size."

FYI: The disarming factor related to eye contact has often caused just enough hesitancy on the part of the assailant for the victim to break free or incapacitate the assailant and then break free or ensure their capture.

- Looking at your assailant also gives you the opportunity to observe identifying characteristics. Experts tell us not to worry about trying to determine how tall an attacker is or how much they might weigh. Instead, use eye contact and visual contact to memorize tattoos, scars, eye color, facial disfiguration (missing teeth, etc.), and clothing.

Upper body including torso, arms, and hands: There are two areas of the upper torso that reveal more about a person's thoughts and feelings than nearly any other part of the body. They are the shoulders and the upper chest.

A person who is on a mission to abuse or attack someone will have their shoulders drawn up stiff and tight. They may be hunched forward out from the neck and jawline signaling they are ready to pounce, or they might be stiff and rigidly in line with the rest of the body to give off the vibes that they are stronger, tougher, and more powerful than you.

The thing you need to be aware of when observing someone's upper chest body language is the rise and fall of the chest, i.e., their breathing pattern. Short, shallow, rapid up and down (in and out) motions indicate rapid breathing. Rapid breathing is associated with aggression and anger. It's as if they are building up steam to power their moves.

The exception to this rule when it comes to possible assailants is when they are in what I will call 'lure mode.' They are trying to lure you into a false sense of security, so their shoulders will be relaxed, and their posture somewhat fluid (even sloppy). But someone planning to use these tricks to inflict harm usually cannot suppress their animosity and intentions enough to slow their breathing, so don't let yourself be lured in.

As for what YOU can do to make sure YOUR upper torso's body language is sending the right message, sit, stand, and walk with confidence—head up, chin out, shoulders square and strong, and stand or sit up straight and tall. When your body says, "Don't mess with me," most would-be assailants won't. They'll move on to an easier target.

In doing the research for this book I read an article on the subject of self-defense in which a police officer was quoted as saying, "...*feet never killed anyone.*" He was referring back to the fact that when someone's hands hover around their waist in a situation involving abusive and potentially dangerous confrontations, it implies the potential for someone to produce a weapon. His point was that when you are involved in a dangerous situation, or if you even believe the potential is there for danger to develop, you need to know where the person's hands are at all times.

We know that a weapon isn't always involved though, so here are a few other important observations you need to make when dealing with a situation in which you might need to defend yourself against someone.

- Balled, clenched fists are a sure sign of aggression. Do everything you can to keep yourself further than arm's-length away from the person in case they try to hit you.
- Someone whose arms are bent at the elbow and who is pointing a finger at you should also be kept a little farther than arm's length away to reduce the chances of being shoved or pushed.

In response, you should always have your hands ready to defend yourself. Using your hands and arms to block, slap or push someone speaks clearly of how you feel about their advances. In order for that to happen though, you need to be mindful of not letting your arms and hands say just the opposite. What does that mean? It means don't fill your arms and hands so full of packages and bags that you send a message that says, "I cannot defend myself." You can avoid this all-too-common mistake by either limiting your purchases to what can be contained in two or three over-the-shoulder canvas shopping bags (than can be used as 'weapons') or make a small investment in a sturdy wagon or cart you can easily pull with one hand.

Legs and feet: Not so unlike the arms and hands, the legs and feet tell a lot about a person's mood and intentions. Their stance can signal if they are about to make an advance. Sometimes it can even tell us how forceful the advance will be. For example, if someone is crouched, slightly bending at the knee and leaning forward, we can safely assume they are going to rush us or throw themselves toward/on us. Or if they are standing tall, with their feet firmly in place and even with their shoulders, we should be prepared for them to try to dominate us in some way (pushing, shoving, pinning us against the wall, etc.).

As for how you can use your legs and feet in self-defense, there are two things you need to remember:

- Look for and take any opportunity that presents itself to kick your assailant. Even if you don't disable them, you will almost certainly gain a few seconds you can use to get away.
- Run. Run as fast as you can toward the largest group of people you can see, the busiest intersection or into the first public building you come to.

The best means of self-defense:

You've heard the saying about an ounce of prevention being worth a pound of cure, haven't you? That certainly is the case when it comes to self-defense. The best weapon of self-defense is doing everything you can to not need it. We also need to acknowledge that things happen that are beyond our control. We can do everything right

and still be put in harm's way. But even then, when we use our body language to speak defensively, and when we use our eyes and intuition to read someone else's, our chances of a favorable outcome raise dramatically. So please, take the time to do these things. Remember: Your ability to recognize the warning signs and send the right messages can give you valuable seconds in which to act; potentially saving your life and/or someone else's.

1: Do a survey among three to six of your friends. Ask them the following questions:

- How often do you walk, jog or go out alone after dark?
- Do you purposefully select a parking place based on how safe it is (well-lit, etc.)? Why or why not?
- Do you make decisions about what you do and where you go based on how safe you believe the location is? Why or why not?
- Would you consider yourself to be someone who is aware of their surroundings?
- If you answered yes, what do you do that supports that answer?
- Have you ever averted a possibly dangerous situation by using body language as a means of self-defense? If so, what did you do?

2: What do the answers to the survey questions tell you about the importance and validity of body language as a means of self-defense?

3: Take the time to watch a few episodes of a crime show or drama such as *FBI*, one of the *NCIS* shows or something similar. Critique the actions of the victims, noting what they could and should have done to try to deter their assailant. Critique the body language of the assailants. What signals did they give?

CHAPTER TEN
CULTURAL DIFFERENCES IN BODY LANGUAGE

"The smile on the face of a radiant bride or a mother holding her newborn child sends the universal message spelled L O V E." ~ Darla Noble

The elderly grandmother of a friend of mine who is Chinese was appalled when she saw a picture of a wedding gown her granddaughter was eyeing for her own wedding. No, the dress's neckline wasn't cut 'down to there,' and no, the price tag didn't equal a year's tuition at Harvard. The problem with the dress was the color. It was white. Glistening, snowy, white.

"Don't worry, Grammie," Celia said to her grandmother. "I want the dress to look just like this one…except the color. It will be red."

Red!?!? Yes, red. Chinese wedding culture and etiquette say that a bride should wear red silk. Red is the color that signifies joy, luck, and happiness—everything you want a newlywed couple to have. It is also the color they believe wards off evil—something else you want every newlywed couple to be protected from. So, red it has been for centuries, and red it still is for the Chinese bride.

The reason I share this bit of information with you is to accentuate the fact that even though we are all deserving of equal respect, opportunities, and life, we are not all alike.

Women are made differently than men. Teenage girls have a different perspective on things like prom and swimsuit season than a grandmother does. Farmers are much more concerned about later than normal hard freezes than a lawyer or fitness expert is, and someone with nut allergies spends more time reading the content label of a package than someone without allergies.

Oh, and here's one more difference you need to be aware of—body language isn't always universal. Darla Noble's quote under the title to this chapter is true. A bride or new momma's smile *is* one of the universal words for love in body language. But it's not all that simple. But then why should we expect it to be? Some of our own body language can have multiple meanings depending on the situation or circumstances. So why should we expect people who speak different languages verbally to speak the same body language as everyone else?

The answer: We shouldn't. And so, we aren't going to go there.

In this chapter we are going to take a look at some of the cultural differences in body language. Unlike previous chapters, though, we are not going to discuss how to respond. We aren't going to do that because the comments after listing each and every difference would be the same: **respect**.

Respect. We are going to learn how to respect the differences in our body language and that of other cultures. And before you ask, here's what respecting includes:

- Taking the time to do a little research on what is considered appropriate and normal body language for another culture if you are going to be a guest in another country or a guest in the home of a person whose culture is different from yours.

- Know what is and isn't appropriate if you will be communicating regularly with a person from another culture—especially if the relationship is professional in nature. You don't want to be perceived as too forceful, to cavaliere or lackadaisical and disinterested.
- Don't make light of or dismiss a friend's body language when it speaks the dialect of a different culture.
- Don't apologize that your body language is different, because when all is said and done, 'different' is a relevant term.
- If you are going to spend much time with someone, take the time to discuss the differences in your body language for the purpose of making sure you understand one another and can communicate without the awkwardness of trying to determine the meaning of something.
- Don't tease someone about their cultural body language.
- Don't pressure someone to conform to your body language. "When in Rome…" does have its place when someone is participating in a dominate culture, but if you expect too much from someone it never ends well for anyone.
- While you certainly shouldn't feel pressured to be someone other than yourself, you need to consider the feelings of someone who might not understand the cultural body language you do by tempering what you do. For example, if hugging is considered too forward

in your friend's culture, don't hug them—no matter how naturally it comes to you.

FYI: The example of hugging is not reserved for different cultures. There are countless young couples whose families are polar opposites when it comes to hugging and kissing…or not. The struggle is real for a lot of young men or women whose significant other's family is more or less huggy-kissy than theirs. Trying to adjust to the exact opposite of what you are comfortable with, without offending your future or new in-laws can be excruciating. So be nice. Be patient. Be respectful. And don't set the bar higher than your loved one is comfortable with.

Matt and Colleen's relationship is a perfect example of this. Matt was raised in a home where both physical and verbal affirmations of affection were all but non-existent. The reasons, which Matt explained to Colleen (and later her parents), were complex and unfortunate. So, while Matt was glad to become part of a family that openly loved and cared for one another, it was not easy for him. He welcomed the hugs from his mother in-law, sisters-in-law, and little nieces. He was thankful and overjoyed that his father in-law showed genuine interest in him, respected his professional skills, and went out of his way to include him in things without putting him on the spot. And when he and Colleen had their son, he made the conscious decision to be that kind of father, too. But it hasn't always been easy. Especially when it comes to hugging, joking around, and inserting himself into conversations (in a good way). But he kept at it and after nearly ten years he is finally getting there. He even initiated wrapping his arms around his mother in-law to express his concern when her father died a couple of years ago.

And finally…

- Don't make a big deal out of something that isn't a big deal. You say *'tomAto'* while someone else says 'tomato.'

Now let's move on to the nuts and bolts of things. We'll start off with something easy; looking at the similarities—body language that essentially means the same thing across the many nations.

- A smile is a smile is a smile….
- People in every culture cry tears of joy, sadness, and pain. BUT in some cultures, crying is considered a sign of weakness and/or is not to be acknowledged or encouraged (especially in men). We'll cover this in more detail later.
- Frowning signifies displeasure no matter where in the world you are.
- An open mouth, dropped jaw, wide eyes, and raised brows says, "I'm shocked!" or "I'm surprised" in every language.
- Tight lips and a furrowed brow are global signs of confusion, disgust, and frustration.

You can't really misread the message any of these expressions convey. But what you *can* miss is the reason behind them—especially when the message is a frown, scowl, one of shock, surprise, disgust or frustration. You may not 'get' that their expression is aimed *at* you, that your actions (body language) is offensive… a cultural faux pau.

That's not what anyone wants, right? Isn't it difficult enough sometimes to communicate effectively and accurately when there are language and cultural barriers? And when you are trying to develop lasting relationships—whether they be business related, friendships, or romantic and familial—don't you work hard to make it not so hard? Yes, and yes! So why not go into things knowing how to make a positive first impression. And then a second, third, and….so forth.

NOTE: The following information is by no means a comprehensive list. And because the world is an ever-changing place with more and more cross-cultural businesses and companies forming all around the world, be careful not to make assumptions. Ask questions. It's always best to ask first rather than have to apologize or make amends later.

Eye contact

- In America, Canada, and most of Europe, making and maintaining eye contact is considered appropriate. Desirable, even. It signifies confidence in yourself and your ability. It also signifies respect for the other person and that you are attentive to what they have to say. But that isn't the case in all cultures—especially exchanges between men and women and exchanges between people you are not closely associated with.
- In African and Latin American countries, eye contact lasting more than a few seconds is considered a challenge of authority and power. It's a way of saying, "Try me…show me what you've got!" The same is true in some Asian cultures.

- In Asia, the Middle East, and some African cultures, children do not make eye contact with their elders, as it is a sign of disrespect.
- In the Middle East, eye contact between men is meant to last and says that they are equals and that the conversation or business being conducted is meant to be taken seriously.
- Eye contact between the opposite sex in the Middle East is brief, at best. Women are strongly discouraged from making eye contact with a man who is not her husband, as it is deemed sexually inappropriate and promiscuous.
- In Asia, Africa, and Latin America, employees are not supposed to maintain eye contact with their employers, or students with teacher or professors. Both are a sign of disrespect and a challenge to their authority.
- Making eye contact in Russia is a sign of respect for the person you are speaking to and shows confidence in yourself. To not make eye contact (in some cases), can be viewed as weakness.

Winking

- In America, Canada, and Western Europe (more so in some countries than others), a wink is often an innocent gesture of communication conveying the understanding that they share secret knowledge.
- In America, Canada, Latin America, and Western Europe, a wink is also a means of flirting and conveying romantically playful feelings.

- In Asian cultures winking is rude and offensive. Eye contact is minimal at best in these countries anyway, so to wink is like adding insult to injury or pouring salt on an open wound.
- Don't wink in Australia. It is considered rude and an act of aggression—one inviting confrontation. It would also be seen as too forward in Eastern Europe.
- Winking is also considered too suggestive and sexually inappropriate in the Middle East.
- In many African cultures, parents use winking to send a silent message to their children to leave the room so that adults can have adult conversations or conduct business.

Hugging

- In much of America, Canada, Latin American countries, and most European countries, hugging between family members, parents/children, and female friends is a common way of greeting. It is not seen as inappropriate or as an invasion of one's personal space.
- In Latin America, some European countries (including Russia), and some Mideastern cultures, hugging is also a common and socially acceptable way of greeting between male family and friends.
- Hugging between female children and teens is common in America, Western Europe, and Canada. Boys, however, are not encouraged to hug.
- Hugging between males after a sports victory is common in most cultures—except Asian cultures.

- Hugging is considered rude, disrespectful, and highly inappropriate in Asian cultures.

Kissing

- Familial kissing is common and acceptable in nearly every culture. Asian cultures, however, are the least emotionally demonstrative cultures in the world. Kissing is not nearly as common or encouraged between people in any type of relationship.
- A kiss of friendship is common even among men in the Middle East, some European cultures (France and the Scandinavian countries, for example), and among women in the European cultures. Most greeting kisses, as they are referred to, are either a quick peck on one cheek or one on each cheek.
- Americans, Canadians, Australians, the British, and New Zealanders just don't 'get' the greeting kiss 'thing' among friends and those you are doing business with. In these cultures it is awkward and can be easily misconstrued. If you don't believe me, think about how many sexual harassment cases you've read about or watched unfold on the news in recent years.
- Asian cultures would never greet a casual or business acquaintance, or even a close friend with a kiss. That is much too personal and invasive of their personal space.
- The British and other cultures who are uncomfortable with this form of greeting subconsciously make it

impossible by keeping enough distance between themselves and the other person to make it inconvenient or even impossible to do.

Personal space

Speaking of personal space…

- Most Latin American cultures, along with the people in India, America, Canada, and Western Europe, stand closer together when talking to one another than some other cultures do. The subconscious and unspoken 'rule' here is that the more familiar you are with someone and/or the more personal the exchange is, the closer you will stand.
- Standing close to someone in these same cultures while talking to them also conveys a message of trust. The people feel safe in each other's presence and are comfortable and glad to be participating in the conversation.
- In the Middle East, women can touch other women in public (link arms, rest a hand on their shoulder to comfort or steady, etc.) and men can do the same with men. But men and women do NOT touch each other in public—not even married couples will be seen in Middle Eastern countries (especially those which are predominantly Islamic) touching each other (holding hands, etc.).

- Japanese people do not touch in public and would never extend a greeting to someone that included touching them.
- Northern European countries are not into touching each other either. In fact, it is rude to shoulder bump, fist bump, clap a hand to someone's shoulder, etc., to greet someone, encourage someone or comfort someone.

NOTE: The exception to these rules, of course, is the parent/child relationship—especially parents and infants or toddlers.

Another interesting thing about personal space and body language in cultures that *do* touch each other and *do* stand, sit, and walk close together is the unspoken rule of status or authority. For example…

Few people would have a problem with their boss or teacher giving them a pat on the back and saying something like, "Great job!" "Congratulations!" or "Way to go!" But not a lot of us would turn that around. In other words, not many people are going to slap their boss or teacher on the back and say, "Thanks for the raise!" "That test was a breeze!" or "How about that promotion?"

The unspoken rule of thumb on this is that it follows a chain of command.

Hand gestures

The body language of hand gestures is surprisingly the most confusing and controversial when it comes to cross-cultural communication. As you are about to see, there is a vast difference in meanings when it comes to things we often take for granted—including the most basic gesture, aka the handshake. And from there the number of differences just keeps growing.

- The handshake—both the firmness and the length of time (number of times you pump someone's hand up and down) can literally make or break a business deal or a relationship. No, seriously, it can!
  - In Germany and other Western European countries, handshakes are usually quick and not too firm. The two...three...or four-pump handshake Americans tend to give seems ridiculous and overzealous to them.
  - But on the other hand, Latin American countries are all about long, firm handshakes. And if you don't want to risk offending them, let them end it. Don't pull away first.
  - The Asian culture, keeping to their belief that touching is not necessary and personal space is to be respected, do not shake hands. They clasp their own hands together or put their palms together (like they are praying), place their hands close to their chest, and bow. Brief, shallow bows are for younger people, deeper bows for older people. And always bow to the oldest person first as a sign of respect.
  - The Asian exception to this is in the Philippines. The people in the Philippines want to shake your hand and look you in the eye, but ONLY BRIEFLY and the handshake

should be LIMP. To squeeze a hand is both rude and a sign of aggression.
- African handshakes should start with the oldest person. But that's not all. The handshake is more of a wrist-shake. Grab the person (loosely) by the wrist and give a few light pumps while asking them how they are doing. Then wait and listen attentively while they tell you.
- Handshakes between men and women in many cultures (including Russia, the Middle East, and Morocco, among others) are considered inappropriate. In some instances, women are not considered equal business associates. In other instances, it is considered sexually inappropriate.
- Another 'extreme' when it comes to handshaking can be experienced in Turkey. In Turkey, a long, firm handshake is in order. It can go on for quite a while because it is a gesture that denotes the level of trust and friendship. The longer the shake, the better the relationship.

NOTE: This is by no means a comprehensive list. You should also keep in mind that there are exceptions to every rule depending on the person's previous exposure to other cultures and the amount of time they have spent living/working in a culture outside their own. So once again I want to encourage you to do your homework and ask questions. Get to know as much as possible about the people you will be working and communicating with so that you can go into the situation knowing as much as possible about how comfortable they are with your culture's body language and what they expect of you in return. And remember: Don't ever hesitate to ask first. No one will be offended when you ask a question meant to honor and respect their thoughts, feelings, and comfort level in spending time with you.

Now let's move on to hand gestures. When talking about body language the definition of a hand gesture is this: *Positioning or moving the hands and fingers in a particular pattern or motion to send a message or denote your thoughts and feelings*.

NOTE: The following images and information have been copied from OERs (open educational resources available on the internet).

The 'thumb's up' is a positive gesture in most every culture. It means 'good,' 'way to go,' or 'I understand.' But in Greece it is a rude gesture that means 'up yours.'

The peace sign is just that—a sign of peace in almost every culture. It also, of course, signifies the number 2 and is a sign for victory. But in Australia and New Zealand, it is a rude gesture that means 'up yours' or 'get lost.'

An open palm held up and out says, "I'm telling the truth," "Wait," "I surrender," or "Hello" in most cultures. To the people in Greece, though, this is also a rude gesture—one that puts an extra emphasis on the phrase 'up yours.'

Talk about mixed signals! In the U.S. this is the widely recognized symbol for the Texas Longhorns football team. In South Africa, Malta, and Italy, this gesture, when pointed at someone, says 'you are protected against danger and evil.' But…in the Middle East it is 'code' for 'your wife is being unfaithful.' Be careful with this one.

In Japan this gesture (especially when the fingers are separated) is a silent insult. To the rest of the world it is simply the number 4.

In most cultures pointing a finger at someone is a form of aggression and considered rude and offensive. In Asian and African cultures, pointing at someone is a serious offense against them. Only dogs and inanimate objects are to be pointed at.

The 'ok' means just that—ok, in Europe, America, and Canada. In these countries it can also mean 'none' or zero. In the Middle East this gesture is a sexual insult. In Japanese culture it denotes coins (money).

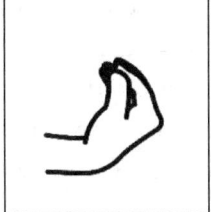
Beckoning someone with your finger or fingers is a simple and quiet way to say, "Come here, please," in America, Canada, and Latin American countries. But in Asian cultures and in Eastern Europe it is rude, offensive, and demeaning.

Sitting and Standing

- We know that sitting cross-legged, with your arms crossed over your chest, or turned partially away from someone sends the message that you are unreceptive and inattentive. The exception, of course, being that of a woman sitting with her legs crossed at either the ankle or knee. We know this is a sign of modesty. These things say the same thing in Western Europe, Canada, and some Latin American countries. But in Asia, crossing your legs is rude and a sign of disrespect—especially when you cross your legs while interacting with someone older and/or an authority figure. In the Middle East, crossing your legs causes the sole of your foot to show, which is frowned upon. Showing the sole of your foot/feet is their way of wishing someone ill-will and bad luck. It is also an omen that something bad is going to happen to you (the person who sees the sole of someone's foot).
- As mentioned earlier (personal space), be mindful of not standing too close to someone. In cultures were men and women don't engage in close friendships or work together as equals, standing too close to someone of the opposite sex can be interpreted as promiscuous or suggestive.
- Do not sit in such close proximity to someone that your legs or shoulders will touch unless you are related or are in an intimate relationship. In just about every culture this is seen as being presumptuously familiar with that person.
- Crossing your fingers behind your back is the symbol for 'excusing' your lie in America, Canada, and some

Western European cultures. Crossing your fingers and showing someone is a way of saying, "Wish me luck!" in those same cultures. But in some Asian cultures (especially Korea), crossing your fingers is a perverted sexual gesture and is never appreciated.

- Covering your mouth with your hand or sleeve/arm when you cough is considered proper everywhere. But in some cultures, coughing is considered extremely rude because it is considered poor hygiene.
- Speaking of hygiene, in China, Japan, Korea, Thailand, Saudi Arabia, and France (among others), blowing your nose is repulsive and extremely rude. You will never see anyone publicly using a tissue or hankie in these countries.
- As inhibited and reserved as Asian cultures are when it comes to touch, showing emotions, and other physical things, they are surprisingly forward in other ways. Specifically, burping/belching and slurping. People in most Asian countries believe that the louder your slurp and burp, the more respect it shows to the hostess. These gestures signal that you are enjoying the meal immensely.
- If you are a lefty in America, Canada, Europe, and most every other first and second world country, you are a minority, but that's all. In many third and fourth world countries, however, if you use or offer your left hand you will be chastised and ostracized. Why? Because in many of these countries the left hand is used for toilet paper. I don't think I need to make any further explanation on this one.

- Dressing casually (gym attire, yoga pants, ill-fitting clothes) is considered the norm in America. But that is not the case in nearly every other country—even those where people have very little in the way of material wealth. When someone goes out in public in most every other part of the world, looking your best, i.e., looking neatly put together and tidy, is the expected normal.
- In most countries people consider talking with your hands in your pocket acceptable; usually denoting a relaxed atmosphere and attitude. But in South Korea and a few other countries, people view this gesture as a reason not to trust someone.

Trying to keep all these differences straight is enough to make you 'do a Dorothy' and make "There's no place like home" your mantra and mission statement. But even if you don't plan to travel overseas, there's a good chance you will need to be at least somewhat aware and astute in how to read and use body language among people of other cultures. So, take the time to at least know the basics.

1: Have you ever traveled overseas? If so, what cultural differences in body language did you notice or encounter?

2: Do you believe people living in the United States should adopt the body language regardless of their culture of origin? Explain your answer.

3: What would you do if you unknowingly made a gesture toward someone that they considered offensive and they confronted you on the matter?

4: How would you handle cross-cultural body language differences with someone you would like to be romantic with?

CHAPTER ELEVEN
HOMOPHONES AND HOMOGRAPHS IN BODY LANGUAGE

"I'll go to the park at two, too." ~ *Any of the millions of third grade teachers in America*

To say the English language is confusing is an understatement. To say it is easy to learn is a lie. Think about it. How much sense does it make for 'y' at the end of a word with one syllable to make an 'i' sound, but if the word has two syllables, it makes an 'e' sound. Except for 'key,' 'pray,' and 'they' (among others)? And what's the case with the rule that if you have a vowel before and 'r' you just say the 'r'…except for words like 'area,' 'organ,' 'ironic,' and 'eraser' (among others…again)?

I could go on, but you get what I'm saying. The English language is packed with homophones (words that sound alike but are spelled differently and have different meanings) and homographs (words that are spelled the same but have different meanings and are sometimes pronounced differently). For example…

- Sew, Sow, and So (homophone)
- Lead and Lead (homograph)
- Fowl and Foul (homophone)
- Win and When (homophone)

- Bat or Bat (homograph)
- Bow or Bow (homograph)

Again, I could go on but there really is no need to, is there?

Here is something else you need to keep in mind—body language isn't much better. Think about it. How many times throughout the pages of this book have you read phrases like, "...except when this or that is taking place," "...unless they are doing...," "You will need to assess the situation leading up to this to determine what is actually being said," or "...depending on the age of the child and their overall mood..."? These are just a few of the reasons that make the statement, "body language is full of homophones and homographs" fair and accurate.

No matter what you think about the matter or how frustrating it is to you, the fact remains that we all need to be able to discern and interpret the meaning of what is being said via someone's body language. Or to put it another way, you need to know if your toddler's hopping around like a wild child is his/her way of saying there's a bug biting them or if they are trying not-so-subtly to say that waiting for you to finish talking to the neighbor really bugs them.

Being oblivious to or uninformed on matters such as these can quickly lead to hurt feelings, animosity between neighbors, misinterpreted intentions aka mixed signals, and costly first impressions.

Despite the truth that it is both impossible and unfair to categorize everyone's body language from one area of the country to mean 'this' instead of 'that,' it is worth spending a bit of time to give you some basic variances between people from different parts of the country. Passing this information along to you will equip you with a little more patience, a better understanding of someone's actions, and a greater ability to accurately read what is being said via nonverbal communication. After all, like Ursula said, we should "...never underestimate the power of body language."

Ignoring a stranger's attempts at casual conversation. People from the northern parts of the country—especially the large cities—along with large cities on the West Coast and upper Midwest usually shun the idea of making conversation with a total stranger. Public transportation, waiting in lines or even greeting the people in your building is not a priority. In fact, to many of these people it is an invitation for trouble and being taken advantage of. They also view this as making themselves vulnerable to being scammed or the victim of a physical crime.

People living in these areas of the country are also of the mindset that they don't have time to waste on casual conversations that will lead to nowhere. They prefer to reserve their conversations for people who matter, i.e., people who can further their career, provide them with contacts and clients, people with whom they want to become friends or romantically involved with or who will appreciate and respect the knowledge, information, and help they have to give.

People who are like-minded and from the same area think nothing of this stand-offish body language. But for people from other parts of the country, where it is considered common courtesy to do these things, it can be difficult to connect. What is normal, safe or appropriate for the northerner and big city dweller is viewed as rude and arrogant to someone else.

So, what body language says, "Save your breath. I'm not interested"?

- Looking away—either over your head, over your shoulder, or in all directions.
- Looking down.
- Turning their body away from you.
- Scowling at you before looking away.
- Burying their nose in a book or newspaper, digging through their purse, busying themselves with their phone, or closing their eyes.
- Walking away without acknowledging you.

If you experience rejection in your attempt to draw someone into conversation OR if you are the one doing the rejecting, here are a couple of things you need to keep in mind.

1. Respect another person's boundaries, level of comfort, and cultural way of doing things.

2. Explain (briefly, because they aren't in favor of talking to someone they don't know) that where you come from (or that the way things are done around here) it's a normal way of life, but that you don't wish to make them feel uncomfortable.

Less hurry and scurry. People from the Midwest and the South, along with people from rural areas across the nation are less inclined to hurry and scurry from one place and activity to the next. They move slower and talk slower. They even take longer to assess a situation and make choices and decisions.

Don't become frustrated with someone who hurries more than you do, or who seems to move at a snail's pace compared to what you are used to. This isn't easy, but if you learn to adjust you will find that you can actually compliment one another.

Likewise, don't misread their pace as a lack of respect for what you have to say/do, or a lack of enthusiasm for being part of an activity. It's a matter of perspective. The hurrier doesn't want to miss out on anything and wants to make sure they get their fair share. The person who takes things at a slower pace is of the mindset that hurrying might cause them to miss out on something important and worthwhile. So, you see, both have the same end-goal. They just have a different plan of action for getting there.

The following movements and gestures will tell you that hurrying and scurrying is the preferred method for getting from point A to point B:

- The person doesn't stop walking when you attempt to talk to them.
- The person may stop walking, but steps in place and does regular 'watch (or phone) checks' to see how much time is being wasted (wasted is their word for it).
- The person puts their hand up as they walk past, indicating they don't want to take the time to stop and listen to you.
- The person turns and goes in the opposite direction if they see you heading their way.

When you observe these behaviors in someone don't try to force them to change. Respect their preferences and personality by calling, texting or emailing them to request a time to speak to them.

Taking plenty of time to stop and smell the roses. People from the South (Texas, Alabama, Mississippi, Louisiana, and so on) are known for being the kind of people who take all the time they feel they need to stop and smell the proverbial roses. They rarely get in a hurry about anything.

Some of their slowness might come from a practical point of view. It's hot and humid in the south, so hurrying and scurrying is only going to make you sweat sooner and more profusely. Taking things slow and easy, on the other hand, is a cooler and more comfortable approach.

Another reason for the slower pace in the south is the fact that they need more patience to do many of the jobs they do. Getting in a hurry doesn't accomplish a thing, so why bother? For example, no amount of hurrying about is going to make the cotton harvest come any sooner or the oranges to ripen any faster. The shrimp aren't going to be ready to catch until well, until they are, and so on and so forth.

Why hurry when hurrying doesn't make things happen any sooner?

The body language of someone who is more than happy to take life at a slower pace is obvious. They:

- Stand and sit with a relaxed posture.
- Walk slower than the average person.
- Speak slowly.
- Rarely, if ever, over-schedule themselves.

- Rarely use or rely on an appointment calendar or date book.
- Are more likely to cook from scratch, garden to grow their own food, and get their exercise through walking, swimming, canoeing, or other slower-paced, low-impact forms of exercise.

So, if you are trying to communicate, do business with or form a relationship of any kind with a person from the south, and you are NOT from the south, be mindful of these simple but relevant facts. If or when you do, you will be glad for the methodical approach to doing things and the patience they have to see things through to the end.

FYI: You might also want to learn from the slower moving southern folks. They typically have less stress-related health problems, which is no small thing.

Enjoy the art of casual conversation. The art of casual conversation—conversation which has no agenda other than to enjoy interacting and visiting with someone else—is an art. Many would justifiably argue that 'thanks' to texting, social media, and social distancing it is a dying art.

Regardless of whether you agree with that 'argument' or not is not the issue here, though. The issue is knowing how to read someone's body language to know whether or not the person you are with is open to shooting the breeze or not. Those who are willing to reciprocate:

- Smile and return eye contact when you begin to speak.
- Turn their body toward yours.
- Stand or sit with a soft, relaxed posture.

- Tilt their head to one side to indicate genuine interest in what you have to say.
- Lean forward (especially if sitting) to let you know they are 'all in.'

Reluctance or possibly even refusal to make eye contact. It is important to understand that people who won't or can't make or maintain eye contact with you usually have a reason other than disinterest or dislike. The reason is often more complex or serious in nature. Sometimes their actions indicate prior or current abuse, a severe lack of self-confidence and self-esteem, intimidation due to feeling inferior or not wanting to get involved.

Putting your finger on the exact cause for their reluctance may be difficult without knowing a little more about the person, but here are a few things you can do to help figure it out.

- Nervous twitching, nervous habits (nail biting, chewing their lip, twisting their hair, etc.), and looking around to make sure they aren't being watched strongly indicates the person is the victim of some sort of abuse.
- Mumbling or giving no verbal response at all, shuffling, swaying or twisting from the waist, or exhibiting a nervous habit shows extremely low self-confidence and self-esteem.
- Drawing their shoulders toward their neck, speaking softly and without looking up, and standing or sitting with slumped shoulders indicates the person is intimidated and feels inferior.

Extremely protective of their personal space. People who are protective of their personal space have a reason for exhibiting body language that says, "Stay outta my space!" The reasons include fear of intimidation, exerting their independence, taking some giant steps toward breaking free of abusive and manipulative relationships, shyness or cultural upbringing (they just aren't comfortable sharing their space).

People who don't want you invading their space…

- Stand or sit behind a desk, chair or other object to keep you from coming any closer.
- Cross their arms in front of them and stand rigidly straight.
- Hold something in front of them—often clutching it to their chest—to keep you at a safe distance.
- Take steps backward to put more distance between you.
- Turn away from you.
- Look away or look down to signal they are done with the conversation or interaction.

Generally speaking, posture and stride (the way someone walks) varies across the country and is based on the overall level of trust they have in each other, their interest in community involvement, and their views on the importance of structured time. This one speaks for itself. You can tell a lot about someone's thoughts and feelings when it comes to matters such as these. Their facial expressions, their willingness to converse, and their overall demeanor tell you ~~everything~~ almost everything you need to know.

CLOSING COMMENTS

"A friend is someone who makes you more than you are, simply by being by your side."
~ Albert Kim

"...almost everything you need to know." That's what you just read. But why just almost? Is it really and truly impossible to know everything you need to about body language? Absolutely! Body language is no different than verbal languages when it comes to context, attitude, the maturity level of the person doing the 'talking,' and the specific situation or circumstances. Or here's another comparison I'm sure you can relate to: How many times have you or someone you know posted something on social media that has been blown way out of context? Or how many times have you or someone you know been bullied and hated on for posting something because *they* (the other person) didn't know, didn't care, and didn't take the time to find out where you were 'coming from'?

It's not pretty, is it? It can hurt—to the point of causing serious and possibly even irreparable damage to an individual or to a relationship. And all because of either a misunderstanding or lack of respect for someone else's beliefs, thoughts or feelings. But before you start nodding your head and making a mental list of everyone you know who is 'guilty as charged' on matters such as these, consider the possibility that you may be just as guilty when it comes to misreading or ignoring someone's body language.

Don't let these things keep you from looking and 'listening' to the body language of the people—both those you are doing life with and those you encounter (randomly and regularly). And don't let these things keep you from using your own body's language to communicate. Body language is both powerful and effective when it comes to communicating. Sometimes it's all we have.

Sometimes there are no words to adequately express how we think or what we are feeling. Sometimes the words won't come because they are being blocked by fear, uncertainty, anger or even discretion; knowing it will be in everyone's best interest if they *don't* speak. Sometimes words are not the appropriate response. Sometimes the person knows that words would do more harm than good and/or that their body language will speak more powerfully than anything they might say.

We've covered a lot of ground between the first and last pages of this book. A lot of what you read may have seemed repetitive. That's because it was. The word 'and' is used in this book 1,404 times. The word 'but' is used 173 times. That's the nature of any language. There are words we use repeatedly when speaking and writing, so why would body language be any different? So, now that we are done I hope you will take what you've learned to heart; using it to be a better communicator—both as a talker and a listener.

www.ingramcontent.com/pod-product-compliance
Lightning Source LLC
Chambersburg PA
CBHW071454070526
44578CB00001B/335